real God

ann ELIZABETH

Ann Elizabeth is the Founder & President of RealOron International Ministries, Inc. ® | www.realoron.org

RealOron® is a ministry dedicated to the destruction of Biblical lack of knowledge, through evangelism and discipleship of all Nations.

Ann has pursued the heart of God and the Souls of Men throughout the years, with direct focus beginning at her supernatural encounter with the Lord; in 2001.

Ann is a dynamic preacher, author, evangelist and teacher of the Word of God.

Real God
Copyright ©2015
By; Ann Elizabeth

No part of this book may be reproduced or transmitted in any form or by any means, electronic or mechanical, including photocopying and recording, or by any information storage or retrieval system, except as may be expressly permitted in writing by the author Ann Elizabeth. Requests for permission may be addressed at realoron@realoron.org.

ISBN Number - 978-1985027701

All Scripture - King James Bible

🖤

Come and experience an outstanding book on the reality of Jesus Christ, and the fact he still makes house calls; enthusiastically reaching down from on high to rescue the blind, crippled, hopeless castaways and sinful nobody's of this world; to place them within his "Family and Kingdom" of Love, Light, Holiness, Purity, Healing and Incredible Truth.

This is an amazing testimony, written about one such encounter. After experiencing severe pain for three years, from a domestic violence episode, in stepped the Savior himself - in person - to love, heal and to inform Ann about the realities of existence, and the root of all evil. Jesus took Ann on an awakening journey, into the Invisible Realm, Heaven and Hell.

Ann relays this story with great exuberance and deep gratefulness, as she longs for every soul to know and to return to their Creator; for their safety and benefit. Please enjoy this beautiful meeting with our God; and see him in a deeper, more focused, intimate level as never before. The

Lord is no respecter of persons. What he did for Ann; he is waiting and desiring to do for you. Never give up, because God loves you and knows everything; about your life, your heartaches, your sorrows and your broken dreams. You can make it, God is for you. God is most definitely, able and available.

PSALM 42:1-2

"As the hart panteth after the water brooks,
So panteth my soul after thee, O God.
2 My soul thirsteth for God,
For the living God:
When shall I come and appear before God?"

♥

JOHN 8:51

"Verily, verily, I say unto you,
If a man *keep* my saying, he shall never see death."

Jesus Christ

real God

PROLOGUE	4
1. THE BEGINNING	10
2. 15 MINUTES	18
3. THE BLUE EYE	22
4. THE MOVIE SCREEN	28
5. THE HEAVENLY ROLLERCOASTER	34
6. JESUS LOVES ANNIE	36
7. THE ANGELIC ARRIVAL	38
8. JESUS THE CHRIST	44
9. THE FIRE & THE OPTOMETRIST	48
10. THE COUNSELOR	50
11. THE SNAKE & THE MIST	54
12. THE DEAD RAISED	58
13. THE HAIR	62
14. THE MIRROR	66
15. HOME WITH QUESTIONS	68
16. GOD APPEARS	72
17. THE EGG	78

18. THE BEAUTY SHOP	82
19. THE STAIRWAY	84
20. HIS MAJESTY	86
21. THE SKI LIFT	88
22. INNER HEALING	94
23. THE CELL	104
24. THE DUNGEON	108
25. ANOTHER PORTION OF HELL	110
26. THE DIRTY FARM	114
27. REBUKING THE DEVIL	116
28. THE WOODEN BENCH	118
29. THE RIVER RIDE	122
30. THE OTHER WOMAN	130
31. THE SATLLITE DISH	132
32. THE HAIRY BEAST	136
33. PONDERING HOME	138
34. THE RAPTURE	142
35. THE AUDITORIUM	144
36. GOD'S PLANS FOR YOU	160
37. THE REPORT	162
38. TO THE ABUSED	166
39. MOVING FORWARD	170
40. GOD'S AMAZING CHARACTER	180
41. IMPORTANT SCRIPTURES	188

ONE

THE BEGINNING

Have you ever heard the word love, and thought you knew what that really meant? Have you ever met anyone that has gone around the moon and back again, to invite you to get to know them; on a very special, intimate level? Have you ever met someone or perhaps you have been someone, who has been mistaken or misunderstood; by the masses at large? Well let me introduce you to someone, who has been waiting for you to meet him, absolutely all of your life. His name is God. This book is dedicated solely to you and to him, as a bridge built for the two of you, to join in complete harmony, love, fellowship and finally; perfect, complete, beautiful understanding. For in this relationship alone, you and God's; you will find love, joy, peace, hope, truth, comfort, goodness, kindness, purpose, passion, mercy, grace, miracles, ability, success, drive, giggles, wholeness and life more abundantly, with eternal life on top of that. Now this is a hard menu to pass up, wouldn't you agree?

I have been a God seeker since childhood. I was always curious about him, and he has been answering my questions ever since. He's been my Father, disciplinarian, coach, savior, trainer, healer, counselor, teacher, authority, comforter, driver, encourager, creator, friend and my complete helper; ever since I can remember. He's seen me through many trials and performed numerous miracles for me, all of my life. He longs to do them for you as well.

I hope you're ready for this; because he is. He started out pretty simple when he first began revealing himself to me, until one day in 2001. Here he came, walking right through my sin packed; adultery laced cottage walls, in person. Who knew; he knew where to find me, in this huge, big; people packed earth? I never met anyone that loves like God. He is not afraid to roll up his sleeves, and enter into filth and confusion; to set the record straight.

His love is relentless, and all consuming. He arrives to rescue, to save and to inform. He never gives up or grows weary. I hope you're ready to be amazingly loved, because this is his person; "Pure Love." I hope you're ready to be amazingly helped; for this is his nature; "Mercy."

I am one of them. I have seen. I have seen his eyes, his face, his arms, his chest, his legs, his laughter and his heart. I was taken into his home. Heaven is the name of that place. I was also lowered into the depths and chambers of Hell. This is the location that was prepared for the devil and his angels; and is also filled with very sad people, who refused to have a relationship of love, humility, understanding, honor, respect and obedience with him; through the Cross of his Son, Jesus Christ. God warned me to leave my life of sin, so I wouldn't end up in Hell, in terror and eternal regret. I witnessed in person, first hand – God's face; of huge sorrow and deep concern, for his entire creation, along with his relentless determination and passionate pursuit, to introduce himself to his creation; and to rescue all from the devil's future, which is "The Lake of Non-Ending, Eternal Fire."

God's deepest desire for you, his beautiful creation; is to spend your life with him here, on the earth; understanding, abiding and remaining in all truth; and living with him in Heaven, when you leave. I pray that what I am about to share with you; will encourage you, fill you with hope and joy unspeakable; and save your life forever, as it has mine. Let us begin the journey.

MEMORIES

I am waiting with delight for the time, when God calls me home, as Heaven is a beautiful and amazing place. The thought of living with the Lord in this location; is very exciting and thrilling. I have excellent taste and the place he calls home, is like walking right into "The Ritz Carlton." Actually Heaven is much finer, but it is a good, visual starting point, for God has truly prepared a life of luxury, for all who love, believe and long to be with him. Jesus states;

JOHN 14:1-3

"Let not your heart be troubled: ye believe in God, believe also in me.

2 In my Father's house are many mansions: if it were not so, I would have told you. I go to prepare a place for you. 3 And if I go and prepare a place for you, I will come again, and receive you unto myself; that where I am, there ye may be also."

God actually resembles the "Michael Angelo" painting pretty well, just in case you might wonder what the Father looks like, excluding the long hair and beard. He stands pretty tall; with broad shoulders, with a heart of absolute gold, and complete determination. His shoes are interesting; and so is his personality.

RELIGION

Many years as a little girl, I wandered around the interior of my Catholic Church; in Evansville, Indiana. I remember admiring the stained glass windows; that decorated the huge sanctuary. This cathedral was dressed with beautifully lit candles, and many ornate statues of the saints. I thought the nuns who served there, were close to God. This impressed me, and I thought about becoming one; for a brief time. It seemed to me that joining a religious order, would be the only way to live close to God, as I loved to just sit and talk with him quite often. I also enjoyed and appreciated the Catholic priests, as they were always so full of love. But the sight of Jesus hanging on the Cross, behind the altar everyday really got to me. I would look at the Crucifix and wish he was alive, and could speak. I didn't know how; he had gotten to be God's Son. I hated the fact he had to die; for what they called "Sin."

I never understood the word "Sin," as this was never explained to me or the origin of "Sin." They simply said that because of "Sin," Jesus had to die.

We attended mass almost daily, as students of the Catholic school. I think we had at least two funerals every week. No one ever told us, where the deceased were headed. As far as we knew, they got stuck in the ground, in a great big box, and that was the end of it. We learned that some people paid the priests; so the dead people wouldn't get stuck in a place, they called "*Purgatory*." "*Purgatory* is middle ground," they explained. They said if we paid God, he might change his mind about what would happen to the person, who just died. They might just escape Hell, after all.

I was always very curious about where God lived. In fact, I asked him this question on many different occasions. He never told me though. I would write him letters and leave them out for him to read, the same way I would leave the letters to Santa Claus; before Christmas day would arrive. I figured God was busy and I didn't want to bother him, so I would write the letters and ask him to take a look, if and when he had the time. I would place the letters on my little white desk that Mom had refinished for me, from a fire sale. I wasn't sure if he would read them or not, but; it was sure worth a shot.

YEARS LATER

Who knew years later, I would see Mom standing before me, in her celestial body; in my "Cottage of Adultery." That's right, you heard it correctly, my "Cottage of Adultery." I'd been married for years at this point and survived successive, ongoing bouts of sexual immorality, pornography, physical, emotional and verbal abuse. My husband had a thing for pornography, from week number two of our union as; "Man & Wife." His pornography always led into physical abuse, after being caught.

My last physical assault came shortly after returning home, from another country with our second adopted child. I had been asleep just a few hours, and suddenly awoke to find him once again, in front of the screen of porn. This eventually resulted in severe physical abuse, to my cranium and body. The attending physicians could only offer compassion, and pain therapy via narcotics, as the damage was completely irreversible. Deep depression sunk in at the thought of never being able, to live a normal life again. I began to seek peace and solace in being alone, as the pain was never ending and always in a continual, forward motion.

I began doing large amounts of drugs, as I was trying to wash down the physical pain and mask the emotional terror, and deep sorrow of it all. I then found myself in the arms of another man, and onto the surroundings of another place entirely. I was constantly praying, asking for God's help; but I didn't know if he would do anything for me, since Mom was left in a cancerous condition; unto her very grave.

I began seeking God for direction. I call it "advice," for this is all I ever thought he gave. I was very Biblically confused. I didn't know where God stood, on the issue of domestic violence and pornography. What would God say to me, if he was to speak? Some issues are cut and dry and some are not; so I thought.

Deep within my heart; I wanted someone to scream out, "It's okay to love "Tex" – just get it together." I wanted this answer, because I was greatly afraid of disappointing God; and I was frightened of leaving my husband, for fear of more abuse.

No matter what I did, I couldn't get rid of the physical pain. I drug my broken body around for three solid years. I hated anyone seeing me this way, especially "Tex" and the kids, as I felt my pain greatly annoyed and aggravated them. I felt that my damage and pain management, were in the way of them having a "normal life." I longed to return to myself, but the cycle kept going, until the Lord showed up; in person.

During the day I laid in my cottage, with various medical contraptions attached to my body, hoping to ease the pain. My intake of poison slowly elevated to; smoking two packs of cigarettes daily, and consuming an ounce of cocaine, and two fifths of tequila weekly. I was a walking mummy, with destructive bandages wrapped around my being, to erase the agony.

I cried out to God continually, *"To Show Me The Way."* I couldn't believe that my life had taken such a huge, downhill slide; into such a deep garbage pen; from the *"Proverbs 31 Woman"* but it did. My only goal was to rid my life completely, of this excruciating physical pain, and find out the answers; I was so desperately in need of. I knew God, was the only one who could help me. I cried out to him, day and night. I always loved God, I always cared about God, and then – I met God; face to face, the one who created; "Existence."

TWO

15 MINUTES

One day while waiting for my sister to come and pick me up; from my boyfriend's house, I heard a voice say to me out loud, "*Kathleen will be here, in exactly fifteen minutes, and you will know that I am talking to you Ann.*" I was alarmed at hearing this audible voice, as it belonged to Almighty God. He was speaking directly to me. I looked up at the clock on the wall, to see what time it was. The clock read; 11:45 AM - exactly.

ISAIAH 52:6

"Therefore my people shall know my name: Therefore they shall know in that day that I am he that doth speak: Behold, It is I."

I remember lying on a massage table, in the center of "James's" living room, with a sock cap tightly fit upon my broken skull. I wore this in order to prevent myself from scratching my head. I rubbed my cranium nonstop, in order to relieve the ongoing, continual pain, as my head was severely crushed. This method of pain relief; over a three year period, about drove me to the brink of suicide, on many different occasions. I was watching the clock tick back and forth, back and forth, when exactly fifteen minutes went by; and my sister Kathleen suddenly knocked at the front door, as the clock ticked; to the very second of what God had stated, confirming the very voice - of; The Almighty.

I was so elated and excited. I actually felt hope and deep relief flood over me, for the first time in approximately three long, hellish years. I knew that God was in the house, and with God comes miracles. God had finally arrived, "In Town." I knew God was bringing change, for God always brings change; in the right direction. God is good and God is love, we can trust him.

I opened the door to see Kathleen standing there and beamed, with a huge grin upon my face. What a wonderful feeling to know that God actually knew; and could see my pain. I couldn't believe he could see me, all the way from his throne in Heaven. I began to tell Kathleen of this event, as we drove home from "James's" house that day. She looked rather amazed, as I recounted the story to her. I felt sorry for my sister, as she witnessed so many years of trauma, abuse and utter neglect. It was really hard on her, to see me in such deep pain. It wore on her a great deal, a very great deal. But I saw sparks of hope fly within her eyes; as I told her the story.

We both knew, that God could do anything. We both knew, that God loved us. We both knew, that God could heal anything or anybody, at any time - hands down. But we both had lived through, the loss of so many things in our lives; including Mom. I always knew deep within my heart, that God would heal me, but I wasn't sure how, where or when he would do this. These were the "mysteries" to me, these were the big "unknowns." But I knew he would; because this is his character, his DNA, his very person. He is not the creator of abuse, neglect, sickness, disease and addiction. That title belongs to our enemy satan and his fallen angels, that dwell in the air here, in people, in Hell and on the land; of the earth.

I began the journey of hope, excitement and anticipation, as I wondered daily how God was going to heal me and set me free, from the locked prison of this physical, ongoing nightmare that I was trapped in; along with liberating me - from the addiction to drugs, alcohol and the like; which had given me nothing but extreme pain and misery. How was God going to bring this to pass? How would he release me, from this Hellish nightmare?

PSALM 103:1-3

"Bless the L<small>ORD</small>, O my soul:
And all that is within me,
Bless his holy name.
² Bless the L<small>ORD</small>, O my Soul,
And forget not all his benefits:
³ Who forgiveth all thine iniquities;
Who healeth all thy diseases."

THREE

THE BLUE EYE

One night I was sound asleep at the cottage, lying next to "James." We were stretched out upon the long - smooth velvet, emerald green futon; in the pitch black of the night. Suddenly I was awakened by a huge, floating, beautiful, loving, blue eye – that stood all by itself in midair. The beautiful blue eye was gently floating around the atmosphere in the room; and slowly came close to me, to squeeze me with love and to gently nudge me awake, at my left shoulder. I knew it was the Lord;

PSALM 32:8

"I will instruct thee and teach thee in the way which thou shalt go: I will guide thee with mine eye."

The Lord had come and appeared, in one of his multifaceted ways. You could just see him smiling from ear to ear. I tried to grab him, but he only beamed. I asked, "Jesus, is that you?" He then shook his head up and down, up and down. He was wearing a huge grin upon his face, and I was so excited to see him. I knew he had come; to help me. I knew he had come; to save me. I knew he had come; to rescue me. I knew he had come; to *finally* free me.

With Jesus Christ; comes love, hope, faith, life, health, joy, peace, truth, acceptance, increase, determination, encouragement, ability, strength, endurance, purpose, responsibility, focus, friendship, discipline, companionship, accountability, warfare, patience, challenge, reason, answers, drive, excellence, missions, sacrifice, commitment, prosperity, refining, change, new life, good and most certainly - freedom. Jesus Christ is the Son of God; what else would he bring? He could only bring what he genuinely is - which is; everything.

I was totally, completely and utterly thrilled to see him. I had waited for him to arrive for three long, hard years. Before his arrival that night, I would pray to him; sing to him, read the Bible to him, write in my journal about him, and talk to my friends of him. Even "James" had been a listening audience, when it came to me speaking about God, as God has always been my favorite subject. There is no one like him.

I would sit out on the waterfront porch of my cottage, as I waited for my deliverance from this mess, in a big, white plastic chair, which was my favorite place in the world to be at the time. I would just sit and stare out at the sea and sing songs of love, and profess how the Lord was going to come and rescue me one day; and then how wonderful it would be, when he would release me from "the prison" of this deep torment, pain, grief, devastation and disease and hopefully the drugs, alcohol and affairs to go with it.

Here is a beautiful description, of Jesus Christ;

JOHN 1:14

"And the Word was made flesh, and dwelt among us, (and we beheld his glory, the glory as of the only begotten of the Father,) full of grace and truth."

I longed to be at home with my husband, while away at the cottage. I longed to be raising our two little children, in the usual way of normal; healthy families. I longed to be pain free. I longed to rewind the clock and wash it all away. I longed to be drug free. I had been drowning myself for so long; in order to wash away the torment, both the physical and the emotional. I definitely didn't know how to reach out to anyone for help; for they weren't God anyway.

What could they really do, but put their compassion on the misery; along with a band aid or two to go with it. For people are just people, they can never do miracles. We are not made that way. We are just the recipients of miracles. God does the miracles. He does these miracles for us, out of pure love, mercy and compassion. People can never take the place of God. For he alone, is the creator of us all; and we live and exist off and through; his very person, in every single way;

ROMANS 11:36

"For of him, and through him, and to him, are all things."

I stared at this beautiful blue eye for quite some time, as it floated and smiled around the room. I then drifted back to sleep, as never before. It had been so many years, since I had slept so sound and peacefully. I was extremely comforted with the fact; that Jesus Christ was in the house. Jesus Christ brings with him; a sense of mystery as well. It is like he is bringing surprises of some kind or another, as he wants you to join him, in this great adventure; called hopeful, gleeful anticipation.

He seems utterly thrilled at the surprises he is bringing, or about to bring; to birth, to fruition, to completion, to being. He loves to create out of nothing and seems deeply exhilarated, about bringing great things to pass for us. I have never experienced anyone that wanted so much for me, and for you. It gives him such great pleasure and personal satisfaction; to do good, for the ones in which he alone has fashioned, formed and created, with his very own; special, unique heart and hands.

He lives to give; for he loves to give, this is his nature. He loves you. He really, really, loves you. He gave himself on Calvary, as a remission for our sins, and to redeem us from the hands of satan; and an eternity in Hell, and to give us a life worth living here. Jesus Christ is still giving; every day of his life; to us, his dearly beloved creation, in every single way. We truly are his priceless treasures, and we adore you Lord; your heart is completely pure.

I informed my sister, that because of Jesus Christ's arrival - she would be witnessing a brand new sister soon. A totally transformed, healed, whole and happy sister. I told her one day, I was going to be able to live a normal life again, like a normal person; in a normal way, without pain and deep and dark addictions, living within the cubicle of painful loneliness; and total demonic isolation and control. I told her that instead of the sad and addicted person I had become, I would one day be dancing with joy, in the healing arms of Heaven.

My sister seemed to be getting excited, about all of this as well. Although, I would sometimes see the doubts of sorrow that would try to fill, flood and invade her heart; as it had been so many long years of agony. I could still see the substance called hope – lying deep within her. I knew God could heal me and I refused to let go of that fact; for he alone was my only hope, and he alone had filled me with this faith I now possessed, so that I wouldn't let go; like Mom did;

HEBREWS 11:1

"Now faith is the substance of things hoped for,

The evidence of things not seen."

FOUR

THE MOVIE SCREEN

A few weeks went by and I was back at "James" house. I would go back and forth from my cottage to his place. I would sometimes spend the night there. One morning after waking up, I saw a movie screen on the wall in front of me. There was a film playing and the set was in black and white. There was no color to be seen at all, in or on the screen. I saw an auditorium full of people sitting in padded, armed chairs, in this black and white movie.

The auditorium was sloped as in all auditoriums, it also had a stage. The people in the auditorium were clapping, and they looked very happy. They seemed like they were clapping for me. I would squint to see clearer, as I have always had to wear corrective lenses, in order to see perfectly. I wanted to get a better view of the crowd; that was displayed before my very eyes. The lens zoomed in on a young girl; that was sitting in a wheelchair.

This young girl had on a dress, which looked just like the one Mom made for me, for my seven year old birthday party. The dress was white, with red polka dots and fluffy, puffy arms - laced with white fabric. What a sight to see; funny the clothing that was worn back then. The lens then zoomed in closer at the girl even further. The girl had on a pair of baby blue wing tip glasses; that resembled the first pair I ever received from my Uncle, who was my eye doctor growing up.

The girl's hair even looked familiar, the hair style resembled the style Mom would shape mine into, for school pictures and was laced with a ribbon as well, right on the crown area. The girl was me. I beamed from ear to ear at this revelation. "How could this happen?" I wondered. "How did God know, what I looked like, when I was a young girl?" "How did he know what dress I had on, and the shape of my hair?"

This was incredible to me. My heart was deeply touched. "How did God even know, I was at "James" house?" "How did God know, where "James" lived?" I had kept it such a big *secret* after all. Who knew that God knows; our *secrets*? Who knew that God knows; every single hair, that is upon our heads?

MATTHEW 10:30

"But the very hairs of your head, are all numbered."

You are never alone; God is always caring for you. Isn't this amazing? Isn't this incredibly precious?

PSALM 33:13

"The LORD looketh from heaven;
He beholdeth all the sons of men."

Who knew that God knew; everything about us? Who knew that God even cared, about every little detail that pertains to us here; upon this earth? He loves us. He really, really loves us. He knows us. He really, really knows us. He made us. He really, truly made us. Think of all the people here upon this earth. There are approximately six to seven billion individuals presently, upon the planet, at this very moment in time. Plus all the centuries, that have come and gone before us. God not only knows every detail of our lives; he knows where we are, every single moment. He knows absolutely everything; even the clothing we wore, when we were little. There are no *secrets*; with God. He knows all; completely and totally. This brings great peace and relief to me, and it should to you as well.

I was mesmerized by all of this, a movie screen playing on my wall; full of people in an audience, clapping for me. These people seemed to care about me. They seemed to want the best for me. I never really knew anyone; that cared that much about me. This was shocking. They were actually cheering me on too. To where, I didn't know. I just knew it was God. God was entertaining me, in my condition with a movie. Precious, isn't it? I felt so alone and hopeless before their arrival. I contemplated suicide, more times than I can recall. I had no friends; only a worn out sister and "James" of course. I had consumed enough drugs to kill a British Army, but God kept me alive, literally – every single day.

Here are the people; in the movie;

HEBREWS 12:1-3

"Wherefore seeing we also are compassed about with so great a cloud of witnesses, let us lay aside every weight, and the sin which doth so easily beset us, and let us run with patience the race that is set before us, 2 Looking unto Jesus the author and finisher of our faith; who for the joy that was set before him endured the Cross, despising the shame, and is set down at the right hand of the throne of God. 3 For consider him that endured such contradiction of sinners against himself, lest ye be wearied and faint in your minds."

This movie played and played for days. I got so used to seeing everyone in the audience and I looked forward to seeing them, every single morning when I awoke. One day, the lens zoomed in on Mom. She looked just like she had, when she had lived upon the earth; to the tee. She was dressed in the red and white striped shirt that she always wore; except in the movie it was in black and white. I couldn't believe I was looking at her, as I buried her seven years prior; of breast cancer. She fought the good fight of faith, but eventually let go of hope; and that is the key to obtaining a miracle. Who knew all these years later, I would be witnessing her resurrection from the dead, and her eternal joy within the gates of Heaven. I was elated to my very core.

The sorrow I had become; was lifting slowly and gradually at being with all of them. I began to feel love and the desire to live again, which was very different and unusual for me. Mom smiled at me, and shook her head in joy at seeing me. She was laughing with glee and you could just tell she was as astonished, at the goodness of God as I was. I believe the ones in Heaven, never stop learning about God. Just like we never stop learning about him here.

He is a beautiful gift; that we continually enjoy opening. I was utterly amazed at God's love and concern for me, as well as his presence there with me. I couldn't believe he had taken the time, out of his busy schedule in running the universe; to help someone like me, a nobody and a sinful lost cripple; hidden away, in a drug induced, *secret* affair cottage. What kind of heart would come, and love a sinner like that? Well, the answer is clear and very simple; the heart of Almighty God;

MARK 2:16-17

"And when the scribes and Pharisees saw him eat with publicans and sinners, they said unto his disciples, How is it that he eateth and drinketh with publicans and sinners? 17 When Jesus heard it, he saith unto them, They that are whole have no need of the physician, but they that are sick: I came not to call the righteous, but sinners to repentance."

God definitely had the right address; he came to save this sinner. Thank you Lord.

FIVE

THE HEAVENLY ROLLERCOASTER

God is amazing. God is supernatural. God is absolute fun; for God created fun. These people in Heaven, on the movie screen, were all on a rollercoaster one day. I witnessed Mom actually riding upon this beautifully, constructed contraption; called, *"The Heavenly Rollercoaster."* She lived mostly afraid, when she was upon the earth. She was frightened of dogs, highways, heights and especially of fast moving objects; especially the ones that would turn you upside down, such as rollercoaster's.

I watched her, as she was riding in this device. She had on a beautiful set of pearls, cascading down around her neck line. She was laughing out loud, full of joy and total glee. She was amazingly free. I was delighted to see joy in Mom. It was a rare quality to witness; as her earthly life had so many years of agony, sorrow and loss. But now; she was in total bliss, and one hundred percent freedom. Who knew that God had rollercoaster's in Heaven? I think he has a lot of fun things up there, just waiting for us;

1 CORINTHIANS 2:9

"Eye hath not seen, nor ear heard, neither have entered into the heart of man, the things which God hath prepared for them that love him."

SIX

JESUS LOVES ANNIE

One night after I settled down, I saw the Lord; very enthusiastically, write these words on the wall behind me, "*Jesus Loves Annie*." I couldn't believe I was reading these words. Here I was all alone, in the location called; "deep loneliness, and heartache," when in steps the Creator; to change my life and heart – forever. His love is irresistible. God truly; loves us;

1 JOHN 4:16

"And we have known and believed the love that
God hath to us.
God is love."

SEVEN

THE ANGELIC ARRIVAL

One day at "James" house, as I was sitting upon the edge of the bed; out of the blue, appeared before me, two bronze, metal pine cone; shaped objects. They came out of nowhere - spinning wildly, at the speed of lightening. They circled and circled in midair, at a rate I never witnessed before in my lifetime. Fast does not relay the speed, supernatural does. They spun right into the shape of a human body. There were two of them that arrived, right before my eyes. Their faces were hidden from me; but not their personalities. They didn't have a face, just an outline like ours. They appeared and landed, right in front of the bed and spoke with great, resounding authority. One spoke, while the other just stood there silently. The one angel said, *"The Lord God Almighty has sent us; to heal you of your pain, if you will let him."*

I was dumbfounded and completely mesmerized. I was totally shocked. I just sat there on the edge of the bed and stared at them both, for quite some time, taking all of this in. I examined them both very closely, with a huge smile upon my face. You would have also; had you seen them. I was so thrilled to have them present, to say the least. "Help and Love" had arrived, right at "James" house. I never knew that God had such amazing creatures. I never knew that God would send them to us; to help and rescue us.

This was truly incredible to me. I felt like the happiest girl in the world, at that very moment; absolutely I did. This was a great distance from being totally isolated, destroyed and all alone; to now this. To have angels arrive, asking me if they could heal me. Unbelievable joy is all I could feel. These angels looked amazingly happy; they also looked amazingly created. They were like fine tuned, precision instruments; of the Lord God Almighty himself. God created; the angels;

HEBREWS 1:7

"And of the angels he saith,
Who maketh his angels spirits,
And his ministers a flame of fire."

They looked at one another and giggled out loud, with huge smiles upon their faces; at my joyful reaction to them. I knew they were glad to see me smile.

God sends angels and God gives angels; to help us;

PSALM 91:11-12

"For he shall give his angels charge over thee, to keep thee in all thy ways. ¹² They shall bear thee up in their hands, lest thou dash thy foot against a stone."

♥

Isn't God Good?

As time went on, I began to have the strength and ability to drive myself. So I would proceed home, trying to salvage the relationship with my husband. But a deep depression was settling in once again; due to the fact of my continual efforts failing, time after time.

"Tex" would always push me aside, no matter how hard I tried. This was very sad and difficult. He never welcomed my presence in the home. I could feel his disinterest and annoyance, upon all of my arrivals. The same vicious cycle would repeat itself, on every single attempt. I would tell him how God was coming to meet with me; and he would just sit and listen, without much interest. I thought he would be happy, but he didn't even blink. The depression that resulted, was enormous. But in the presence of the angels; the depression would lift.

The "If Angel" stood there, and waited for my response. But I was silent, so he asked again; this time with greater joy in his voice, "The Lord God Almighty; has sent us to heal you of your pain, if you will let him." I said, "Yes!" So I lied down on the bed, as I had done so many times before, for physical and medical treatments. One angel stood to my right, the other angel stood to my left. The one on the left had to stand in the bed;

he actually went right through the bed. It was so amazing to see these angels. God has made some amazing things, and they are definitely one of them.

They began to work on me, at the speed of lightening. They had instruments; that went around and around my body, at a very extreme; fast paced rate. They were cutting bands; off me. These bands would fly into the air, and land onto the floor. They were black in color, and the width and length; of a thick belt.

When I went later to grab one of them; they vanished within my hands. These bands were spiritual and invisible, to the human - naked eye. They were the devils cords, that he had tied around me; as I had gone into his territory and domain; called "Sin" - and was his captive, as a result;

PROVERBS 5:22

"His own iniquities shall take the wicked himself, and he shall be holden with the cords of his sins."

There are no words, to describe the way I felt at that moment, no words at all. I felt awe and relief flood my being, as I was now in the hands of the one who longs to protect and free us. The one who loves me; the one who loves you. His name is Jesus Christ. I could weep at the memory of this, and many times I do. God came to help me. God came to love me. God came to heal me, and God came to deliver me; from the devil. I was and am so utterly grateful; beyond words. When man didn't have the answer; God did, he always does. No man could do anything for me; so here was God, with his loving, "Heavenly Team."

The physicians informed me; that I would always live in pain as there was, "*No Cure*" for me. But God and his mighty angels changed those words, within minutes. The "Heavenly Team" looked magnificent, and excellently designed by none other; than God himself, and Jesus Christ. That is the only way to describe them. These angels were first class, in every sense of the word. I felt like I stepped into a beautiful dream; one moment in the ash heap, the next moment - in awe.

EIGHT

JESUS THE CHRIST

As the angels were working, I looked out of the corner of my eyes to the right, to see someone very special standing there. This person had on a long, white robe and it was non-other than Jesus Christ himself. He was standing right in the middle, of all places; in "James" kitchen.

Jesus Christ has brown hair and a beard, and a huge heart full of love. He wore a very concerned face, and his eyes were amazingly powerful. I couldn't believe he was standing there; a monumental, huge relief describes the emotions that washed over me. I beamed from ear to ear, he did too. He looked serious; very serious. He looked like he had a huge mess on his hands, and that mess; was me;

LUKE 24:36

"And as they thus spake,

> Jesus himself stood in the midst of them,
> And saith unto them,
> Peace be unto you."

I was so much at peace to see the Lord. He has a pair of unforgettable eyes. When you look at him, you know that you are looking at God himself. You know he is; "The Creator." You know he is; "The Risen Messiah." You know he is; "The Savior of All," who will believe in him.

The power contained in those eyes; was hard for me to stare at, for any length of time. I had to look away often, as my body couldn't contain his supernatural energy.

The angels continued with their work, as they were really making progress. I could feel my body lightening up, as well as tasting blood going down my throat. This was quite alarming and I whispered silently to God; "God, they are going to cut my throat."

Immediately, a very small; tiny angel with golden hair and a diamond encrusted, pink dress flew in. She was adorable. She was about three inches tall and roughly one inch in width. She was very lively and full of absolute joy, energy and fun. The Lord spoke, "You watch and follow her with your eyes, and you will be fine." I was shocked, "God had color?" I never thought about that kind of stuff before, I never realized this. The thought just never occurred to me, about the things God made. I would usually just talk to God about every day, normal life. I never took an inventory of what he owned, or possessed;

LUKE 2:40

"And the child grew,
And waxed strong in spirit,
Filled with wisdom:
And the Grace of God was upon him."

We grow, as Jesus grew. Funny how much patience; is in God's cells, but I saw the reason why. God wants us to be safe with him; forever. This is his absolute DNA.

NINE

THE FIRE & THE OPTOMETRIST

The angels stopped working for the night, and I fell asleep. The next morning I awoke to the angels, this time they had fire with them. They began informing me; they were going to run fire from the top of my head; down through the souls of my feet. I said, "Sounds good to me." So here came the torch of fire, and they did as they said. They ran that fire; right through the center of my body. The fire felt warm, and very good. I assumed they were healing; the frayed nerve endings, that ran throughout my spinal column. Given their credentials; I didn't ask any questions.

I then saw the Father; walking back and forth beside me. I just beamed as I watched him move. It was extremely comforting to know, that he was there and that he was in charge. It is quite an amazing thing, to gaze upon the one who created all of us. He looked like he was deep in thought, and up to something very serious. I didn't worry though, you could tell he had it covered. I then fell asleep, for the evening.

The Lord was there in the morning to greet me. He came in a physician's white coat, and had an optometrist's machine with him. He asked me which side looked better; the right eye verses the left, which lens looked clearer to me.

I was amazed at him. He is fun to be with, this is for sure. I answered him as we went through the process, of the *"Eye Exam."* He was showing me how we see with the natural eye; unless he opens up our retina to see into the unseen - invisible realm; the dimension containing himself and his "Heavenly Host."

He was slowly unveiling the mystery; the divine mystery of "The Gospel and the Afterlife," for my knowledge, safekeeping and protection. Heaven is one of the highest, greatest beauties ever witnessed; and Hell is one of the lowest, darkest, saddest places; you will ever know. But the choice was clearly being unveiled to me, over a process of time. Thank you Father God. Thank you for the very, clearly seen; choice.

TEN

THE COUNSELOR

One day the Lord arrived and began to ask me questions about my, "Accident" - as I would call it. I never used the word "Beating." I didn't like the word, as I wanted to forget the whole ordeal. I longed to forget what happened, to me. I also knew "Tex" seemed at times, very sorry for what he did. I didn't feel that beating him over the head for the past, was the proper way to handle the situation. I wanted and longed to forgive him, and I did forgive him - many times. I just desired so deeply to be free of the pain, no matter what the price was, no matter what the cost. But I was killing myself in the process; with my own blind, "deliverance and personal, chosen healing methods." That being drugs, alcohol and the illicit, on-going, sexual relationship with "James."

Jesus Christ began asking me, "*So, tell me what happened?*" I would then begin the story, and I noticed I began to speak; about a hundred words per minute. This was new, as the prison of pain had taken a toll on my verbal and social skills. I would imagine a prison of despair and isolation, might do this to just about anyone; taking the joy out of every single piece of you; slowly, steadily and methodically, one day at a time; one hour at a time, and one minute at a time. The factual and actual slow descent of your life; into utter hopelessness and a life held and bound; within a prison - without an escape. This is a very hard life to live; and to endure.

The prison of ignorance, sickness, disease, sin and abuse paralyzes and destroys you. This real, hellish cell - is a horrible place and an absolute, desolate existence; that I desire for no one, and neither does God. I gave the Lord every little detail of, "*The Episode.*" He is actually the only one, who has ever heard the full story. I was a firm believer, in covering another's sins, at any and all costs. I never delighted in gossip, especially about my husband; for we were as one, at least in my own imagination. We had been a union of a very happy, successful type; so I thought.

The Lord would listen to me, as I would share with him the details of the incident, and then he would very calmly and very gently respond with, "*Oh, and what were you doing; before this?*" I felt a gentle prodding in my heart; knowing my guilt. I would recall a personal episode of sin, as I sat there with the Lord. He would just let those thoughts sit in the air for awhile and then we moved on to his next question, "*So, go on and then what?*" So I with glee; relayed to him, all that "Tex" had done to me; very emphatically, to say the least. It was a relief to have someone, to talk to.

The Lord would listen; and then he would go back to the question, "*So, what were you doing, before this happened?*" Then, the gentle knowing in my heart; of my sin, would just sit there. Then; time would suspend in the air, with the calm knowing and understanding of my guilt. The Lord really wanted me to get that part, he really did. For that part is extremely relevant; and highly important, in all of our lives.

The Lord wasn't ignoring what "Tex" had done, he actually never commented on it. The Lord was focusing; on me. The Lord wanted me to speak and get it all out, for the very first time. He wanted me to know, that he knew and he wanted me to know, where I had gone; "The Wrong Way," so that I wouldn't suffer; from those mistakes again. The Lord stated *"The Blame Game,"* didn't work in the Garden of Eden, and it wasn't going to work here either; or anywhere for that matter. The fact is; without the acknowledgment of our sin and the repentance of it; there will be no forgiveness or remission of our sins; and death will be the result; which is a real, dreadful and horrific location; called - Hell.

The Lord is full of gentle, non-compromising authority. The Lord is God. The Lord is holiness, purity, righteousness and absolute truth; with a genuine and total love, commitment and real concern for every living thing; in which he has made under Heaven. This is him; this is his DNA. The Lord always leads his people; in the right way, the honest way. This is called righteousness; and the path of the righteous, is called "Life."

ELEVEN

THE SNAKE & THE MIST

One night at "James" house, I looked in the mirror to see my eighty five pound body frame, with sunken dark eyes staring back at me. I was startled and sickened; by the reflection I was witnessing. Many times my skin would even turn different shades of yellow. I thought I probably had cancer, like Mom did. My hair was even falling out; at an alarming rate, leaving huge patches of holes on my skull. I looked like a walking disease. I was a very sad sight; to behold.

Later on in the evening, my sister arrived with some food. I told her, how I was more than likely; going to be deceased soon. She just looked at me with that look of hers; and she actually just kept moving forward; about the business she had arrived for; and that business was my nutrition. She wanted to fatten me up; for good reason, as I did look a great deal like Mom did years before – very thin, bony and gaunt.

I lied down on the couch; to get some needed rest, after my sister had gone for the evening and all of sudden, there stood Jesus Christ. He was full of joy, full of excitement, full of animation and full of life. He had a huge, beaming grin upon his face; showing me a few things about existence. He was revealing to me; how he had stood with his heel, on top of satan's head; and crushed it.

He deeply hates, and despises Lucifer. The Lord emphatically notified me; with great joy and much excitement, that I would be following suit; and do just as he had done. I sat on the couch, amazed at his presence and his teaching. The Lord is a great teacher, and I loved being with him;

ROMANS 16:20

"And the God of Peace
Shall bruise satan under your feet shortly.
The grace of our Lord Jesus Christ be with you. Amen."

Shortly after that, a white mist appeared above me. It looked like a big, white fluffy cloud; and it landed right on the top of my stomach. I heard the Lord speak, *"This is the Holy Spirit."* I was thrilled to have the Holy Spirit consume my body with his presence, and his much needed power. A healing and impartation was taking place, and I could literally feel it. What peace; I experienced;

JOHN 7:38

"He that believeth on me,

As the scripture hath said,

Out of his belly shall flow rivers; of living water."

TWELVE

THE DEAD RAISED

The Lord is so very tender, compassionate and extremely merciful. He feels our every pain. Sometimes the deep pain of emotional despair, or the pain of the physical or financial losses we find ourselves in; with no help or hope to be found anywhere; makes us cave into, the deepest ditches of isolated prisons, that we genuinely feel; we will never, ever exit. We feel this for good reason, for very good reason. For without the intervention of Almighty God, we would never make it out – period. There would be absolutely; "*No Way Out.*"

I retreated as usual, to the bedroom for the night. I turned the lights out and was about to get into bed, when to my total surprise and elation; Mom appeared right before my eyes; right out of nowhere. This was not the movie screen on the wall. Mom was actually there with me in person, standing right before my eyes; standing directly in front of me.

I could tell she was so happy to see me. Her face glowed like a diamond, and the joy in her, was like a fountain that poured forth nothing, but living love. She beamed with excitement and joy, at being able to be there with the Lord; to help me. She began running around the room, filled with joy unspeakable and full of total glory, life and enough zeal to arouse any sad, lonely or lost carcass anywhere. She was moving all her body parts, and was shining and glittering; like a pure diamond.

We have skin care lines, that truly achieve amazing results; upon continual and consistent usage of them. They exfoliate our flesh, and we do glow. But I have never seen anything quite like this, in my entire life. Her face resembled a diamond, full of sparkling light and glistening all over. She looked exactly like she did, when she was on the earth; but better - much better. She seemed very joyful. She was absolutely and totally; free.

Her personality, was the same. She was still my kind, beautiful - loving Mom. But she was feisty, and full of zeal as well. What a privilege for God to be so good to me, allowing me to see all that I was seeing, and to know the certainty of truth. What an honor, to say the least. Mom was fascinating to watch, after I got over the initial shock of seeing her. I bet God was standing there with a huge grin upon his face, at my reaction to all of this, as I had never seen the dead raised; until this very moment; except for Jesus Christ. What a beautiful sight, they were to behold. God has brought forth many other people, from their graves as well;

MATTHEW 27:50-53

"Jesus, when he had cried again with a loud voice, yielded up the ghost. 51 And, behold, the veil of the temple was rent in twain from the top to the bottom; and the earth did quake, and the rocks rent; 52 And the graves were opened; and many bodies of the saints which slept arose, 53 And came out of the graves after his resurrection, and went into the holy city, and appeared unto many."

"Death" never looked so beautiful;

1 CORINTHIANS 15:55

"Where, O Death is your Victory?
Where, O Death is your Sting?"

♥

THIRTEEN

THE HAIR

I fell asleep that night, with an angel smiling at me. He was sitting in the bed, with my head in his lap. He had a huge smile, upon his face. He was truly beaming, from ear to ear. It is not often, to my knowledge; that God allows one to see their "*Unseen Helpers, and Protectors,*" unless the person really needs it. This angel was bigger, than most professional football players put together. He was very well built. He had dark black hair, and looked like he worked out regularly; in a gym. His biceps were very large, and his chest was very well; developed.

I loved seeing the angels. Their presence made me feel; very safe. They looked like they would destroy, absolutely anything; that might try to harm me. As I gazed around the room that night; I could see many of them just sitting there. They were all wearing blue jeans, and tee shirts. God knows that I lived in blue jeans and still do, as they are one of my very favorite; clothing pieces. I felt safe, I felt protected; I then fell asleep.

The next morning after awakening, I felt like I needed to kneel down upon the floor; which was a rare habit for me, ever since leaving "The Catholic Church." I knelt down and began to tell the Lord, how much I loved him; as this love I felt, overwhelmed and flooded my heart and soul. This love was consuming my being, and I was naturally responding to it. As I knelt there, I felt the Lord come close to me. Upon reaching me, *the Lord extracted one single hair from my head; and the pain I had* continually experienced, for a period of three, solid years - *vanished*.

I began to laugh with joy, and utter amazement. I began to laugh at God's incredible, supernatural ability; *to end our pain*. He does this out of pure love; for us. The pain had been like a sharp dagger; that was stuck inside a solid position, within my right eye. This pain continually pulsated; at an annoying, ongoing; never ending rate. But here he came, Jesus Christ and just like that; pain gone. The pain left, at one touch of his hand. Exciting, isn't he?

MATTHEW 9:20-22

"And, behold, a woman, which was diseased with an issue of blood twelve years, came behind him, and touched the hem of his garment: 21 For she said within herself, If I may but touch his garment, I shall be whole. 22 But Jesus turned him about, and when he saw her, he said, Daughter, be of good comfort; thy faith hath made thee whole. And the woman was made whole from that hour."

♥

Who better knows how to fix us, than the one who made us? The repair is a healing and restoration process, and we come out of it; better than before. Don't you think we are fortunate, to have him as our "Creator?" We can definitely pride ourselves; in him. We can have and hold this pride over his being, abilities, character, integrity and his very person.

Do not allow anyone to steal your admiration; of God. It is ours; to have and to hold forever. We will actually live with him, for the next zillion times, a zillion years and more. The number is infinite and unending. It is called; *"The Endless Life"* – *"The Eternal Life."* We will run, fish and laugh with him; forever. Maybe we will walk with Peter on the water, or race on it for that matter. We will be supernatural like him. We will be; out of the flesh.

FOURTEEN

THE MIRROR

I began to pray one morning, after getting up from a restful night's sleep. I knelt down and heard the Lord speak; he said, "*Grab your hand mirror on the bed, and stand up.*" I had kept my hand mirror on the bed beside me, as I often looked into it quite often. As soon as I knelt down, I noticed a pair of feet had arrived right behind me. The pair of feet; wore a dark brown pair of sandals, with all toes showing. The toes even had hair on them. It was the Lord. I stood up as he requested and then he said, "Look into the mirror." I thought this was strange, as I didn't have a mirror behind me, to see any reflection. But to my amazement; when I looked into the mirror, I could see my entire back. I could also see him standing there.

He had a device in his hand; that looked like a piece that belonged to a vacuum cleaner. It was the piece you take, and go around the home with; in the corners and close to the baseboards. The Lord began to tell me, that he was going to operate on my back region, and not to be alarmed or afraid. I watched on, while he took this instrument; and began removing the skin off my back. I could literally see the interior, of my back and spine.

I didn't get squeamish; which was shocking for me, as I am not the *"medical type."* He then proceeded to take this instrument up and down, the interior of my back; straightening it, and repairing all the nerve damage that I had. He was also aligning the spinal column. I could feel the surgery, as there was a light sensation of pain. But the three year, chronic pain in the spinal area; was *vanishing*. I then watched him, as he placed my skin back onto my back, directly on top of the muscles. I was dumbfounded at his ability. But he is *"God, The Creator, The Healer and The Great Physician;"*

1 PETER 2:24

"Who his own self bare our sins in his own body on the tree,

That we, being dead to sins,

Should live unto righteousness:

By whose stripes ye are healed."

♥

FIFTEEN

HOME WITH QUESTIONS

By now "James" was a thing in the past. God had taken his place, and God was with me all the time. I began to want nothing whatsoever, to do with "James" in any way, shape, form or fashion. I just wanted to go home. I longed to be home, with my family. I loved my family, I loved my home. My physical pain was gone now, and I was ready to begin again with "Tex," and take care of our small children. This would be a resurrection for me, as I hadn't enjoyed life or been absent from pain, for three solid years. I was so excited at the thought of picking up my children, and holding them in my arms. I would smile with joy, at the thought of it. My heart was filled to the brim with thanksgiving to God, for setting me free; of my physical prison.

I began fixing myself up again. I began putting on makeup and trying to make my hair look half way decent; at least what was left of it. I tried going back home, but to no avail. I would walk into my house every time, and find "Tex" very standoffish and extremely arrogant. Cold is a good adjective, for the demeanor he had. I would attempt to sit down with him, at the dining room table; and inform him of the Lords visits with me, and the way that he was healing me. I shared with him my desire to live in my home, with him and the children. His response was nonchalant. He didn't care what I wanted. He wanted me, "To go on with my life," as he would say.

I even tried sleeping, in my own bed one night. His response was, "Get out. I don't want you here anymore." I was in shock at his behavior. I got up, got dressed and drove away; very, very sad. Here was God; in person – repairing a broken body that he had mangled, with his own two hands and he didn't care. He wanted me; gone. He wanted me; out of his life. This was very hurtful to me, because God was going out of his way to repair my broken body; and our fragmented, dysfunctional home. "Tex's" demeanor added to my sorrow, more than words can say.

I then went out and purchased more drugs, to ease my pain. I could sense God's great displeasure, at this point. God knew I was back on, "The Cycle." The cycle of numbing my pain from "Tex's rejection," in the usual way that I would, walking right back down the road marked, "Destruction."

Remember what the angels said to me, when they arrived? They said, "*God wants to heal you, of your pain; If you will let him.*" See the problem? My antidote and only solution to all of this real and deep wounding, was to erase it. God's answer; was to heal it, without the tools of the devil; which were drugs and the like;

PSALM 147:1-3

"Praise ye the Lord: for it is good to sing praises unto our God; for it is pleasant; and praise is comely. ² The Lord doth build up Jerusalem: he gathereth together the outcasts of Israel. ³ He healeth the broken in heart, and bindeth up their wounds."

God wants to bind up our broken, wounded and ravished hearts. While satan wants to destroy us, with numbing agents. Let us choose; God. Let us choose; "Life." God is able.

SIXTEEN

GOD APPEARS

The darkness appeared once again the following night, as I lay there alone and in silence; in my cottage. But someone else appeared, and that someone else's name is God. Out of the darkness, light appeared and many bright, beautiful colors. I could see the angel's walking and spinning around the room, then I saw Mom.

They were all strolling around the atmosphere with happy, brightly lit faces and then another walked in, that I hadn't clearly seen before. He was tall, broad shouldered and had a high waist, with long legs. He was very well dressed. Dignity and honor; describe him best. He had a look upon his face, of deep concern, great displeasure and sorrow; at seeing me in this blind, sad, lost, sinful and hopeless condition. I knew he was God the Father, for he looked like a Father, where Jesus looks like the Son;

JOB 19:25-27

"For I know that my redeemer liveth, and that he shall stand at the latter day upon the earth: 26 And though after my skin worms destroy this body, yet in my flesh shall I see God: 27 Whom I shall see for myself, and mine eyes shall behold, and not another; though my reins be consumed within me."

I just loved watching God walk. He has the best posture. He had on a beautiful, dark maroon, velvet suit, white cuffs and beautiful white gloves. He looks like he works out in a gym. He is in very good physical shape. He has very good taste in clothing, as he dresses impeccable. He eventually took a seat on the futon, the green - velvet one. I tried grabbing him around the waist, in order to hold him; but my arms went right through him instead;

JOHN 4:24

"God is a Spirit."

God is not of physical matter; but of spiritual matter. An example of physical matter or substance; is a wall. An example of spiritual matter or substance; is a bubble. I began to cry as God sat there, on the green, velvet futon with me. I decided to try to hold him, around the waist. I couldn't feel his structure. I could only see it. I sobbed and sobbed as I laid there, within his arms. I never thought I would stop crying. I was so glad to see him. I was relieved that he was there.

He just sat there, and let me cry. I must have cried for about an hour or so. I eventually looked up at him, and to my astonishment; I saw that he was wearing a big, jeweled crown upon his head. I never envisioned him, as one who would wear a crown. I stared at it for a second or so, and looked to my right; I then saw Jesus Christ lying there, in his white robe beside me, with blood all over it;

REVELATION 19:13

"He was Clothed with a
Vesture Dipped in Blood:
And His Name is Called,
The Word of God."

After seeing Jesus Christ lying there beside me, in his bloody vesture, I looked back up at God and spoke these very words, "You didn't heal him either?" What was I thinking? Crazy, isn't it? But we are not born with knowledge. We learn and continue to grow, just as the Bible states;

1 PETER 2:2

"As newborn babes, desire the sincere milk of the word,
That ye may grow thereby."

Growing means to learn about God, and to follow his word and commandments; with certainty and understanding; every single day of our lives.

The blood on Jesus; represents his blood that he shed for you and me, on Calvary. His blood; is what remits my sins. His blood; is what remits your sins. Remission means; the release of the bondage, imprisonment and penalty of sin; which is death. Jesus blood was placed upon the mercy seat; before God, after he rose from the dead. This was done in order to reconcile us back to God. Jesus purchased us back from the devil, to make us his own; and to restore a relationship between us and the Father.

Calvary (The Cross) is the only bridge that God built, between man and himself. In order to reach the Father, we must go to and then through; "The Cross; which is Jesus Christ, The Lamb of God." Without this process, you will never enter Heaven; to God's sorrow.

Evening was settling in and all of a sudden, I noticed this beautiful blue light going around and around my fingers. This blue light was making rings around my fingers, like a wedding ring. Then a beautiful long banquet table was set before me; and there appeared before my eyes, many of my relatives sitting in tall back chairs. They were mostly the women, in my family heritage and genealogy. They began saying one to another, very excitably, "*Annie Married Jesus, Annie Married Jesus.*" What this meant, was that I had become a part; of "The Bride of Christ; The True Family of God."

"The Bride of Christ" are God's true, faithful, beloved, holy, sanctified, consecrated, committed people that are truly his; upon this earth. The "Bride of Christ" are people that love him, serve him, honor him, respect him, apologize when needed, stay with him and obey him; all the way, to the end of their lives. These people belong to him, in every area of life. For these people, God is their life.

Heaven was bringing me *an invitation* to belong to them, just as the Bible states;

MATTHEW 22:9

"Go ye therefore into the highways,
And as many as ye shall find,
Bid to the marriage."

This statement or decree of me being a part of "The Bride of Christ," seemed very much off the mark; for I was a lost, confused, broken and sinful person; which was truly obvious. But when God comes along with his amazing grace and teaches you, equips you, leads you, loves you and makes you; you actually become what he has decreed; to your astonishment, thanksgiving and utter delight. He calls things the way in which they shall be; not the way they currently are, as the Bible states;

ROMANS 4:17

"God, who quickeneth the dead,
And calleth those things which be not, as though they were."

♥

God does miracles; he changes people, and he was changing me;

2 CORINTHANS 2:14

"Now thanks be unto God,
Which always causeth us; to triumph in Christ,
And maketh manifest the Savour of his knowledge by us,
In every place."

♥

I fell asleep.

SEVENTEEN

THE EGG

The next day God took me into the unseen, invisible realm of existence. There are two atmospheres in life, the visible and the invisible; just like the Bible tells us;

COLOSSIANS 1:16

"For by him were all things created, that are in heaven, and that are in earth, visible and invisible, whether they be thrones, or dominions, or principalities, or powers: all things were created by him, and for him."

I don't know if this was actually Heaven itself, or someplace God created to exist; for a moment in time and space, just for me. He can create wherever and whenever he desires; for he resides in absolutely no box, and he is without limits. He is uncontainable, and uncontrollable.

Upon entering into this atmosphere, I found myself in a very beautiful, formal exquisite room. The surroundings resembled an egg, right out of an elegant jewelry store. The walls of this room were made of beautiful gold and green, thick velvet fabric. The walls were not straight like our walls, they were elegantly curved. There were also couches made of the same fabric; that sat attached to the walls around this expanse.

The walls were not dead, and flat like our walls. They sparkled like diamonds, glistening with light beaming through them. I walked around this room, taking it all in. I never experienced such beauty in my life. I ran my hand over the soft, plush fabric, and felt the smoothness of its fibers. I then decided to lie down upon the floor, and look at it from that view. I actually began crawling across the room, to see it all. This place was a work of extraordinary beauty.

I was all alone in my enjoyment of this expanse, and then God walked in. He had light beaming, right through his legs. He has very strong *pillar like*, thick long legs. He walks in complete, and total authority. It was as if great power; was coming right through his being. At the very moment he walked in, a black slimy creature ran from me; it was as if this thing, ran right out of me. This black slimy thing; was running from Almighty God. I then heard God speak; *"satan, be gone from her!"* I was alarmed, nauseated and sickened, at the sight of this thing; running right out of my body.

What was so amazing; was the fact, I didn't even realize that demons existed. But they do. I had just witnessed one of them; running right out of me, and away from me; at that very moment. Demons are the fallen angels that refused to obey God, and for that reason; God threw them out of Heaven. They now live upon this earth with the human race, as the Bible clearly tells us;

LUKE 10:18

"And he said unto them,
I beheld satan as lightning, fall from Heaven."

Some demons also dwell in Hell, as the Bible informs us;

2 PETER 2:4

"For if God spared not the angels that sinned, but cast them down to hell, and delivered them into chains of darkness, to be reserved unto judgment."

The demonic kingdom has government, rulers and rank. They are wicked, ugly and offensive to the eyesight. God wants all to know of their existence; for if we ignore them, they will destroy us. If we do not stop fellowshipping with the demons; knowingly or unknowingly, in the activity of "Sin," we will be destroyed. If we ignore the devil, "The Prince of the Power of The Air," we will abide in the Lake of Fire; for all eternity;

EPHESIANS 2:2

"Wherein in time past ye walked according to the course of this world, according to the prince of the power of the air, the spirit that now worketh in the children of disobedience."

After witnessing this slimy, filthy demon; I do not comprehend how they received the title, "*Prince*" to anything whatsoever. They are full of absolute raw hatred. When you think of a "*Prince*," you think of royalty. Just the opposite, applies to their lives. They are of the lowest scum, of material substance; I have ever seen, with my own two eyes. They are raw evil. They are cursed. The devil is a God hater, an angel hater, a good hater and a people hater. They live to deceive, and to destroy mankind; both here and eternally.

EIGHTEEN

THE BEAUTY SHOP

I was then transported and taken, into a very beautiful beauty shop. I knew this was in Heaven. I saw many work stations there, just like we have upon the earth, only so much more colorful, bright and interesting. The whole place, glittered and sparkled. There were big hairdryers, sinks and the like. I remember sitting on the sidelines, and watching all of the angels, and the people that were present. I was so thrilled to be with them, in this beautiful location. I really needed some beauty treatments. I felt this was God's way of telling me; that it would be done. Jesus Christ was running around with total glee and great, unbridled enthusiasm; as he was giving me this special tour. Here is Jesus Christ;

ISAIAH 61:3

"To appoint unto them that mourn in Zion, to give unto them beauty for ashes, the oil of joy for mourning, the garment of praise for the spirit of heaviness; that they might be called trees of righteousness, the planting of the Lord, that he might be glorified."

Jesus Christ was ecstatic, to take me on this tour. He was filled completely with utter joy, at my being there. He wants us to know of the beautiful future; that await all, who will obey and remain with him, unto the end;

JOHN 17:24

"Father, I will that they also, whom thou hast given me, be with me where I am; that they may behold my glory, which thou hast given me: for thou lovedst me before the foundation of the world."

I so enjoyed being with the Lord, and taking in all of the sights. I was truly amazed at all I saw. I absolutely just loved being with them. It was quite the opposite, from all the years of isolation, pain and loneliness that I had experienced. I never wanted to leave this place. I felt safe and greatly loved.

NINETEEN

THE STAIRWAY

The next atmosphere I found myself in, was a stairway; within a palace. I was gazing out of this beautiful, ornate window on top of the stairs, from a side ledge. I was looking at some amazing scenery; very picturesque. The angels began telling me, that I would be putting on a wedding dress soon; and would be escorted inside one day. I wanted that day to be that particular day, the present day; but to no avail. The angels also mentioned the fact, that my smoking had to go, or I would not be allowed; to enter into Heaven.

I didn't like what they were saying; but they were telling me the truth, the absolute truth. I knew they were hoping I would make the important, necessary changes that were needed in this area of my life; or look what the result would be, as the Bible clearly tells us;

REVELATION 21:27

"There shall in no wise enter into it anything that defileth,
Neither whatsoever worketh abomination,
Or maketh a lie:
But they which are written in,
The Lamb's Book Of Life."

I shrugged off the angels words like water after a shower, like it was no big deal. I had no desire or intention whatsoever; to ever, absolutely ever, quit this so called, "*Habit*." I regret that choice, for it truly cost me; to the bone.

TWENTY

HIS MAJESTY

The tour continued on, and what a beautiful place it is. I was standing in a certain location on the ground; and looked up to behold Jesus Christ, as he was walking up these beautiful ivory; stone steps, with quite an entourage of people following after him. I was witnessing what is called His Majesty;

2 PETER 1:16

"Eyewitnesses of His Majesty."

Now you have to remember my Catholic origin. This was phenomenal for a Catholic's eyes. I thought Jesus Christ, was a very poor carpenter. This mentality is wrong. He is the Son; of Almighty God. He is the Creator; of Heaven and Earth. Some Catholics, actually believe that poverty is holiness. This mentality is wrong. Poverty is directly related to and from;

satan himself. Please do not buy into this lie; of the devils. The one where he tells you; "God wants you; poor." God wishes for all to be in good health and to prosper, even as ones soul prospers; as the Bible clearly tells us;

3 JOHN 1:2

"Beloved, I wish above all things that thou mayest prosper and be in health, even as thy soul prospereth."

I love the word wish here, I think it is precious. God wants all; safe. God wants all; with him. God wants all; to be whole, healthy, free and prosperous.

TWENTY ONE

THE SKI LIFT

I found myself one day, flying in this contraption with God. It was white and had a huge window in the front. It also had huge windows on both sides, made of solid glass. Inside of this device, were seats like the interior of a bus. The bus driver on the ski lift was Almighty God, and Jesus Christ was sitting right behind me. We were flying over different portions in Heaven. I was so thrilled to be taking a drive; with the both of them. I loved watching God maneuver this contraption. He was sitting pretty high up, and to the left. He kept his hands on the wheel; the whole, entire time.

He let me gaze around the atmosphere, and take in all of the sights. At one point while driving through the galaxy, he went right around the stars in the sky and spoke, "Annie, one day I am going to throw you out there, and you are going to be a star." I just looked up at him and smiled. I felt bad for God, as I knew he wanted the very best for me. But I thought he obviously; wasn't seeing me in my true, current, horrible condition. I was the furthest thing from the definition of a star, of any kind - whatsoever. But this is what he meant, when he spoke those words about me being a star. They are found in the Bible;

DANIEL 12:3

"They that be wise, shall shine as the brightness of the firmament; and they that turn many to righteousness, as the stars forever and ever."

What a project, I have been for God. But God loves projects. God loves people, God loves you and he changes us; from glory to glory, as the years progress and unfold;

2 CORINTHIANS 3:18

"But we all, with open face beholding as in a glass the glory of the Lord, are changed into the same image from glory to glory, even as by the Spirit of the Lord."

As we were flying over one particular area, I happened to look down to my left; to see a round fireplace, with a stone seating area encircling it. The fireplace had a screen on it, like the ones we have here and use upon the earth. There were also chairs placed in a circular fashion, right around the fireplace location. I noticed a few people sitting there by the fireplace, and they were reading out of some book. I couldn't tell what book it was. I could just see how very devoted they were; to their studies. Little did I know at the time; what all of this meant, but it is stated in the Bible as well;

MALACHI 3:3

"And he shall sit as a refiner and purifier of silver: and he shall purify the sons of Levi, and purge them as gold and silver, that they may offer unto the Lord an offering in righteousness."

God was informing me that sanctification; was right around the corner. Sanctification is where you learn from "The Word of God, the Holy Bible," and obey it. This is where you sweat when you read the Bible, and find out; the absolute truth of life. This is where you run away from sin; with all of your heart, might, mind, and soul. This is where you run away from the consequences, and future of sin. This is where you discard and throw away; the old, former life - that was saturated in nothing but dirt, debris, satan and sin. This is where Jesus Christ sits on top, of the whole entire process, cleansing out his beloved sheep, his beloved creation, with pure love and deep; consistent, ongoing concern – which never ends.

As we were flying through space, passing over the fireplace area; I heard Jesus Christ speak these words very firmly to me, "*Don't look back!*" This is exactly what the angels said to Lot's wife years before, when she had escaped out of the wrath of God; that was about to land within the lewd, sexually immoral City of Sodom and Gomorrah; just as the Bible states;

GENESIS 19:17

"And it came to pass, when they had brought them forth abroad, that he said, escape for thy life; look not behind thee, neither stay thou in all the plain; escape to the mountain, lest thou be consumed."

Jesus Christ was warning me of the consequence, of returning to a life of rebellion and sin. I heard that warning very loudly, and crystal clear. Jesus Christ is truth, and he wants us to believe; in order that we live, and not perish.

There is sad news to report about Lot's wife, as she didn't heed the angel's warning, and she looked back at her old life instead. She chose to disobey God, and was destroyed as a result; just as the Bible states;

GENESIS 19:26

"But his wife looked back from behind him,
And she became a pillar of salt."

Believing God will save our lives. We need to believe every single word he has written for us; in the Bible. His Word is there; for our knowing, safekeeping and protection - both in this temporary state upon the earth; and for all the ages yet to come. Eternity is way too long for the rebellious, it never ends.

God finally landed the ski lift and pulled right up and into, a portion of a mountain. He turned around to look at me, and spoke these very words; *"You are going to park up here with me, in the cleft of the rock; but don't forget the music!"*

EXODUS 33:22

"And it shall come to pass, while my glory passeth by, that I will put thee in a clift of the rock, and will cover thee with my hand while I pass by."

The music God was talking about, was praise and worship music; for God inhabits the praises of his people. Praising God makes you strong. Praising God helps you to fly on the wings of the wind, through horrendous conditions and packs of demons. Praising God changes you. I was so thrilled to be with God, but then all vanished. I found myself back in my cottage - alone. I was very sad to be back upon the earth. But God has promised to never leave us, or forsake us;

HEBREWS 13:5

"He hath said, I will never leave thee, nor forsake thee."

TWENTY TWO

INNER HEALING

The next day God arrived at the cottage, and wanted to do some inner healing. I thought, "Why bother with that stuff, of all things? Isn't there anything a little more fun, and adventurous to do?" I was one to always run from the counselor's office, at a pretty fast speed; as they only gave advice and never changed a thing. They would smile, take notes, hand you kleenex and take your money, lots of it usually. And you would leave there with the same old bag; full of problems, with little to no results. My motto was, "Just toughen up, and go on. There's no other choice." I'm laughing out loud; and that is good for all of us, just as the Bible tells us;

PROVERBS 17:22

"A merry heart doeth good; like a medicine."

The Lord ignored my personal request, to skip the inner healing. He directed me to stand right in the center of the living room, of my cottage. He began to target damaged emotions and memories, at an alarming rate. His aim went for the things; I had tried to bury and forget, through the years. It was as if he threw his supernatural arrows - right into the center, of a deep wound and the arrow would pierce – the traumatic disaster point. Then God's super abundant healing would arrive; right into, the pool of pain.

As this was happening; I fell to the ground sobbing uncontrollably. This would last for a very long period of time and then refreshing showers of clear, pure water - would saturate and bathe, the very interior of my soul. Sometimes, a black spirit would run from me, as God targeted the wounded and inflicted area, which was deep within me.

The devil attaches himself to our pain, our trauma, our psyche and our very soul; our person. satan enjoys feeding us; his poison of hating a person, our lives and ourselves. He longs for us to inflict pain upon our beings, and has nothing to offer but lies, despair, depression, remorse and suicide – just to name a few of his appetizers.

When God heals these wounds, the devil is history. He can no longer park, abide and dwell where the pain was; in the location where he continually fed himself, upon our wounds and living on them - for breakfast, lunch and dinner. The devil and his "bride," the great whore, enjoy our sorrow and pain deeply; as stated in the Bible;

REVELATION 17:6

"And I saw the woman drunken with the blood of the saints, and with the blood of the martyrs of Jesus: and when I saw her, I wondered with great admiration."

Can you see the truth? Do you understand the hatred the devil has, for all of us? It thrills his soul to inflict pain and disease, upon all creation. Then he loves to blame it on God; as he tries to turn our hearts against God, in order to destroy us. This has been a never ending cycle, from the beginning of time.

The emotional healing went on all day long, and into the wee hours of the night. I became extremely fatigued, and exhausted. Every time I wanted to sit or lie down upon the green, velvet futon; I would begin to itch. This itch would aggravate me, to the point of having to get back up and stand upon my feet; in the center of the room. This was a big hint from God; to remain standing, for he wasn't finished. He wanted me whole, completely whole. God doesn't specialize in anything half way. Complete wellbeing, freedom and wholeness; is the only goal he has in mind, for all of us. He only gives what he is – *"Perfection in Love."*

Well, I had enough of the inner healing; and decided to take off. The only place available to go that early in the morning, was to "James" house; as it was roughly 1:30 AM. I began my journey across the town, in my big black Land Cruiser and drove right through the city's downtown, nightlife district. Everyone was out partying on the streets, and in the bars;

totally intoxicated from one substance or another. I - out of the blue, felt a boot go right up my seat. I looked up into the rearview mirror, to find God sitting in the back seat; with a very serious look upon his face. He didn't budge. He didn't move. He didn't blink, nor did he smile; no matter how much I longed, for that response from him. He just sat there straight faced; informing me that he was there, and that he wouldn't be vacating any time soon. God does not leave any job halfway done, or unfinished. He is there to see the project through; to the end. We; are that project;

PHILIPPIANS 1:6

"Being confident of this very thing, that he which hath begun a good work in you will perform it until the day of Jesus Christ."

Perform here is the Greek word *epiteleō*, which means to bring to an end, accomplish, perfect, execute, complete. Can you see God's goal; for each one of us? He wants us whole. He wants us complete. He wants us free. He wants us safe, and nothing else will do. We are on the road, going into his image; through Christ;

GENESIS 1:27

"So God created man in his own image, in the image of God created he him; male and female created he them."

I gripped the steering wheel tightly, after seeing God's unhappy face in the rear view mirror. I pulled up to "James" house and surveyed the place, and found it completely and totally deserted. I ran through the forsaken, abandoned dwelling; and found absolutely no one present, whatsoever. "Now what?" I thought. My heart was pounding, at an all time high. I knew God wasn't happy, and was sitting in the backseat of that truck of mine; waiting for me to enter. What a situation; a very, very sweaty one at that! "Oh well," I thought – I'll just drive on back; to the cottage.

I kept eyeballing God, in the backseat. He wasn't a happy camper, and this was making me squirm; filling me with high anxiety. I pulled up to my front door, after making it through; the throngs of drunken people downtown. As I saw them, I thought, "You're not going to believe who is in my backseat. You would never; ever be acting like this - if you knew - who was riding with me, at this very moment in time." I was sweating profusely; within a state of total panic, and extreme terror.

I finally parked my truck, and sat there for a few moments. I was hoping that I might be the only person; inside of that vehicle. I didn't hear anyone exit, nor did I hear the back door slam shut. I then jumped out of the truck, and slammed my front door. I thought God might have left, due to the fact I didn't hear him exit. But as I turned around; after exiting the vehicle – there stood God - in crystal clear view. I screamed bloody murder, took off running and locked my cottage front door. A few seconds later, there he stood; right in the middle of the cottage. You cannot lock God out, for God is Spirit and walks right through material substance; such as walls, cars, boats, etc.

You cannot; outrun God. You may have outrun your earthly father, but not this one. You may have "outsmart" your earthly father, but definitely and most certainly - not this one. God is fast; very, very fast and extremely quick. He had come; to save my life. I just did not realize it at the time; whatsoever. I thought he had only come to heal my body; and emotions, and then go back to Heaven; with the angels. I didn't know; "*The Way, The Truth or The Life*," at all.

The inner healing continued on, into the wee hours of the morning. I then was finally able to fall asleep. I was completely drained and totally exhausted. God did quite a lot of work on me. I wonder if he was drained as well. I sure would have been. I kept wondering who was taking care of the entire world; when God was there with me. I didn't realize at the time, that he is *omnipotent*; and completely everywhere at once. Here is the definition of the word *omnipotent*: Almighty; possessing unlimited power; all powerful. The being that can create worlds, having unlimited power; of a particular kind; as omnipotent love.

Time elapsed and the inner healing seminar; was finally over. I was glad and extremely grateful. I was drained from crying, and seeing all these black shadows run from me. I even witnessed a black snake lying on the floor, all coiled up; right there in front of me. God wanted me to know the facts of life – the facts and the certainty of; - *The reality of the devil*. All of my life, everything was about "*Good, God and Jesus.*" I never heard or learned much, about the *devil*. The things I had read about him in the Bible; I would shrug off and discard, as non-important information. God was beginning to teach and explain to me – *life*. He began teaching me, the things I wanted and longed; to ignore. satan was one of those things.

I was lying in bed one night, on my green - velvet futon; listening to music and here came God. He said, "Tonight, we are learning about how "*Sin*" entered into the earth." I said, "Okay." Then he began running up this hill, and sat down. He began telling me of the snake, the garden and the lie. He was very sad this happened. He told me how this caused dirt and pain, to enter into his creation; that being mankind. I didn't want to discuss these things with God. I had greatly enjoyed the beauty of Heaven, the magnificent angels, the egg, the beauty shop, the ski lift ride, seeing Mom, seeing him – all of it. But this was a closed subject to me; but not to God.

Moments later there appeared upon the ceiling, a circle above me. God began to speak to me, about how I needed to know; "*The two sides, of the story*." There was a bad side. There was a devil. Then I saw his face; *The devil's face*. He looked very sarcastic, very sinister; completely and extremely evil. He owns a seething, deep hatred for all humanity; worldwide. This was written upon; and over his entire, morbid countenance.

We then went on to, "*Holding Your Position - In The Hard Times*." God was the coach. He would have me squat and hold that position, for very long periods of time. He was building up my strength, and endurance. I assumed this was for my body, as I hadn't worked out for years. But first the physical aspect, then the spiritual;

1 CORINTHIANS 15:46

"Howbeit that was not first which is spiritual, but that which is natural; and afterward that which is spiritual."

♥

God would make any navy commander; look weak in comparison to him.

This was very hard, very strenuous and at times; completely annoying. But when God is in the house; God is in charge. This is sometimes, to our flesh's agonizing hatred of it. We actually scream out loud, or seethe deeply from within. Sometimes that scream is only a long, slow breath and/or moaning. Sometimes it is a very loud shout. God then adds a touch of joy, and lots of grace, for you and I to be able to swallow it all; and go on. It seems like this process; never ends.

God then showed me *pink birds flapping around together*, in a pool of water upon the ground. He said, "*You can be one of them, or you can be an eagle. If you are going to be an eagle, you will fly with me and you will have to stand alone; but I will be with you.*" After witnessing the *bird bath*, the way they quack at one another and quarrel; I then decided, I wanted to be an *eagle*. Actually, I believe God always had me enrolled in this program. I was just the one; not aware of it.

I was tired and I told him, "We are done. The training is over, and I have decided that I am going home; with you - now. I want to go home to Heaven. I am done with this." I then matter of factly, packed up my purse; which was completely laced with cigarettes. I then looked at him straight in the eye, and thought I would call the shots; from that point on, because I was totally and completely drained, fatigued and exhausted. I was finished. I was done.

Well, God never sleeps; nor does he slumber;

PSALM 121:4

"He that keepeth Israel, shall neither slumber nor sleep."

God has supernatural energy, and we are encased in this contraption called a body; that actually gets tired and irritable. I know God knows this, for he alone has made and fashioned us. I know Jesus Christ recalls vividly; the years of being in his body, while upon the earth;

JOHN 4:6

"Now Jacob's well was there. Jesus therefore, being wearied with his journey, sat thus on the well: and it was about the sixth hour."

God said, *"Well, we are now going to move on, to somewhere else."* I guess he thought he would speed up the teaching a bit, as I had never been to *Bible College*. He didn't have much to work with; as the years of physical decay and emotional insanity, had gotten the best of me. What I had learned and known at one time; of the Bible, had gradually seeped out of me. God warns us in the Bible, to not let this happen, for the destruction of our lives, will soon follow;

LUKE 19:26

"For I say unto you, That unto every one which hath shall be given; and from him that hath not, even that he hath shall be taken away from him."

Death will follow; when we ignore putting *"The Word of God"* into our lives; on a daily basis. We are a people; that leak. Death; is satan.

TWENTY THREE

THE CELL

I then found myself in a place; that was totally disgusting and extremely grotesque, in every single way. I was in a cell;

1 PETER 3:19-20

"By which also he went and preached unto the spirits in prison; [20] Which sometime were disobedient, when once the longsuffering of God waited in the days of Noah, while the ark was a preparing, wherein few, that is, eight souls were saved by water."

This cell was lined with bricks. These bricks were not clean bricks. These bricks were dark, slimy and trashy bricks. These bricks were covered in; cobwebs. I heard a noise above me. The noise was made from several bats that were flying in midair. Here comes a great promise in scripture; to remember, after seeing this mess;

DEUTERONOMY 28:44

"He shall be the head, and thou shalt be the tail."

You will be the head, not the tail; above and not beneath, *if* you obey God.

This was a great place, if you are a *witch* I suppose. It looked like *"The Halloween Nightmare."* This location looked like the place we went as children; for that *"Holiday,"* unless your parents knew better. They may not have understood the reality of *"Halloween,"* being a creation of satan himself. Please do not get angry, with your parents. Did they create; the galaxy? Did they know; all things? Only God and God seekers know; the important and vital things of life. God's extremely concerned about you knowing; and embracing with both arms, *"The Facts of Life,"* that have been placed in *"The Bible,"* for your knowledge, safety and wellbeing.

This is the love and heartbeat; of Almighty God. There is only safety and protection for your life, in the knowledge and obedience of the scriptures. We as *Catholics* were in, *"The Holiday of Halloween"* full force; as the candy was free, and big bags of it. With all this sugar, "Who cared who started what, at this point?" But now is the time, to begin to care. For your very life depends on; *"The Knowledge,"* you gather from *"The Bible," "The Knowledge you retain of The Bible,"* and *"The Knowledge you obey from The Bible,"* until the very end; of your life;

2 THESSALONIANS 1:7-9

"And to you who are troubled rest with us, when the Lord Jesus shall be revealed from Heaven with his mighty angels, 8 In flaming fire taking vengeance on them that know not God, and that obey not the gospel of our Lord Jesus Christ: 9 Who shall be punished with everlasting destruction from the presence of the Lord, and from the glory of his power."

As I was standing in the cell in Hell, I heard the Lord speak. He was standing on my left. I could almost feel his emotional state; as he knew, I was not aware of this location whatsoever. The Lord was very gentle, and kind to me. Then the Lord spoke, "*The spirits that deceived Eve, live here.*" That is all he said; at that moment in time. His words just hung out, in space. I was thinking to myself, "The spirits that deceived Eve?" And then I recalled, "*The Bible Eve.*"

I was in shock to be standing in Hell, absolute shock. I was alarmed to my very core. I had never entered into this location, in my life. I never even studied the place; nor did I really believe in it. I never acknowledged it in any form, or fashion. But now, I was standing smack dab within the center of it, taking in the most abominable sights. These sights were of pure raw disgust; and utter filthiness, to the lowest degree.

Do you realize this is the last place, God wants any of us to end up in? But the problem, the huge problem is this. Unless we seek and embrace God; obeying and keeping his ways and commandments, we will all end up there; to God's great sorrow, and certainly to ours as well. This is what God wants *all of us*; to know, realize and accept; from his heart of gold and deep concern. We must learn to be his children, in complete love, submission and obedience to him. This is the answer; the only answer, given to mankind. Then, onto growing up and maturing; into his image.

The devil deceives. The devil lies; and the devil misguides creation, on an ongoing basis. He leads creation; away from "*God, The Bible, The Way, The Truth and The Life.*" He leads creation in seduction, disguise, deception, doubt, delusion, discouragement and ignorance. He also leads creation in defiance and rebellion, just like his. He does this in order to destroy our lives here, and escort us into Hell forever; when we die. He hates us; and wants only destruction for us. He is a friend to *No One*. We all reap what we individually sow. We end up; where we chose. Please avoid Hell. Obey and remain with God, to the end.

I wondered if God was going to leave me there – in Hell, for good that day. I was cringing at the thought of it. I didn't want to be stuck there forever. It was a horrible place. Fear was rapidly running, through my veins. I deserved *Hell*. I truly did; as I was a non-repentant, consistent, ongoing "*Christian Sinner.*" But God had mercy on me. Then The Lord spoke, "Ann, you do not have to come here. But, you have to go to my Cross." I thought, "Thank You God, not a problem; I will find one, as soon as I get out of this place," and that was final.

TWENTY FOUR

THE DUNGEON

We then vanished and appeared at yet another location, in Hell. This one was outside of "*The Dungeon.*" There was a stone, concrete wall; standing right in front of me. It was about one hundred feet in width, and fourteen feet in height. Located to the right of the wall, was an arched, dirty, concrete doorway. The Lord was standing beside me, to my left. He began informing me, of the name and keeper of the location. The name of the place was *Hell*, and the Keeper of the location was *satan*. satan was standing outside his, "*Dungeon Hell Hole*" as I looked on;

LUKE 11:18

"If satan also be divided against himself,
How shall his kingdom stand?"

I could hear people screaming in torment, on the inside of this place. I could tell it was very hot, and extremely miserable. It seemed like the interior walls of this cave, had people attached to them; in chains. The Lord told me how the devil gets his people, and takes them in there; to torture them; for all time. I was appalled and in deep shock, at the information I was seeing and hearing. I then stood up straighter after hearing this information from the Lord, and very matter of factly; marched right over to the devil and screamed loudly; "How dare you do this, to Gods people." We immediately vanished, from that location;

HOSEA 4:6

"My people are destroyed, for lack of knowledge."

♥

TWENTY FIVE

ANOTHER PORTION OF HELL

The next place I found myself in; was on top of another portion; of Hell. I can still picture the location, like it was yesterday. All forms of evil were all over this environment. Demons of every size and shape were swarming around, to and fro; at a rapid pace. The space was nothing but complete disgust, dirt, fire and filth. Almighty God was standing on my right, and Jesus Christ was standing on my left. We were located above a huge opening; looking downward into the interior of Hell. Then God spoke, "*One of us standing here, is going to Hell. It will not be me, and it will not be my Son.*" Well, the only person left; was me. I was scared to death, and began to scream for help. Just then, demons began clawing upward to scratch and torment me, in a vicious and raw manner.

I was very disgusted, and full of agonizing fear. My heart felt like it would pump - right out of my chest. I couldn't believe that God would send me to Hell. Fear once again gripped me as never before, as I saw satan running up towards me - to grip my throat, between his dirty claws. I continued screaming at the top of my lungs - for God to save me, from these demons and this place. satan is a supernatural, psychopathic killer; literally. He lives, dwells, functions, resides and works, inside of the invisible realm of life.

The devils aim, goal, and purpose; is *"The complete and total destruction, of each and every one of us."* He is no respecter of race, religion, origin, talent, beauty, economic, sexual or social status. He could care less, whether you are religious or an atheist, a freemason or in the secret illuminati group, in a Bible Study or a porn shop. He longs to deceive you; right into the chambers of Hell itself;

REVELATION 12:9

"satan, which deceiveth the whole world."

The Greek word for *deceiveth* is planaō - meaning to cause to stray, to lead astray, lead aside from the right way, to be led aside from the path of virtue, to go astray, sin, to sever or fall away from the truth.

Do not allow satan to deceive you. Stay in *"The Word of God - The Bible,"* daily. Live by *"It Is Written,"* nothing else. Walking with Christ is a life long relationship. If you walk away from Christ; you will walk right into the arms of satan, and Hell will be your *"Forever Home."* If you do not return to Christ before you die, Hell will be your *"Forever Home."* satan sits back and waits for people all over the globe, to walk away from Christ. satan does this through offenses, jealousy, fatigue, problems, stress, time delays, aggravation, heartaches, disappointments, injustices or anything he can come up with. satan loves to accuse God to us, for the pain in which he alone; has inflicted upon us. Please resist and ignore the devil and stay close to Christ; always, and unto the end;

REVELATION 12:10

"For the accuser of our brethren is cast down,
Which accused them before our God, day and night."

The next minute things subsided, and I could see objects from a distance. God was still at my right hand side. I was then closely looking into another portion of Hell; very clearly. In one section there was a man in a wheelbarrow. He was actually a very ugly demon. Some demons look like people, they look like us. This demon was smoking on a pipe, and driving around on a wheelbarrow. There were huge, ugly, dirty - steel firepots steaming; and there was a fire burning within them. There were also various fires going on, in several locations. The place was full of haystacks, with an abundance of straw. This brings to mind a specific scripture;

1 CORINTHIANS 3:11-13

"For other foundation can no man lay than that is laid, which is Jesus Christ. [12] Now if any man build upon this foundation gold, silver, precious stones, wood, hay, stubble; [13] Every man's work shall be made manifest:

for the day shall declare it, because it shall be revealed by fire; and the fire shall try every man's work of what sort it is."

Hell is severely dirty and gross. *Hopeless* is the word, and ongoing condition there. These people are prisoners; forever. While the rest of the world goes shopping, cleans their house, does their nails, takes their trash out, cooks a meal, takes a shower, does the dishes, fixes a flat, does their laundry, gets the mail, goes to the dentist, gets their haircut, fills up their gas tanks, goes to the park, walks their dog, pays their bills, swims at the beach, goes for a bike ride, walks to school, drives to work, goes to the gym, strolls through the mountains, takes vacations, have children, get married, graduate from college, attend a funeral, etc., the people in Hell are there, and being tortured; forever; because they refused to know and obey God, while they were here upon this earth; during their very short lives. What a horrible way to spend; all of your eternity. Now is the time to know God, and obey him forever; Amen? Please allow God to protect you, through Christ; from this place.

The demon on the wheelbarrow in Hell - kept looking at me with his sickening appearance, very sinister indeed. He was licking his lips, at the thought of my arrival; so he could begin the non-ending, torture treatments; upon my very being - physical, mental and emotional torture episodes. Their abuse is a cycle - of *Non Ending Torture*. Hell is the absence of God, who is all good.

TWENTY SIX

THE DIRTY FARM

I then noticed we had moved, into another realm of Hell. This place is where I saw demons; having sex with animals. It was completely dirty, foul, repulsive and putrid. These demons were located on the outside of a fence, of some kind or another. It looked like an old wired fence. There was someone there riding a horse, in a cowboy hat, jeans and boots, with a lasso. They seemed to be enjoying themselves immensely, as they were giving me the grand tour. This someone was the Lord, who was pulling me around in a small red wagon; so I could take in all of the hideous sights. I witnessed perversion and depravity being committed there, at an all-time high. Then I saw demons, people and animals, having sex with one another. I wanted out of this place, and I wanted out quickly.

EXODUS 22:19

"Whosoever lieth with a beast, shall surely be put to death."

♥

TWENTY SEVEN

REBUKING THE DEVIL

I then found myself back at my cottage, and the Lord spoke; "I am going to show you; what you have allowed into your life, with your very own eyes." He then opened my spiritual eyes; for me to see my cottage, for what it looked like in - *The Unseen, Invisible Realm*. There were demons present; of every shape and size imaginable. They were everywhere, gawking at me. They totally filled the expanse of the cottage; from wall to wall, and filled the place from floor to ceiling. There was not a space, where they were not present. The place; was packed.

God then sat down next to me, and spoke; "*Why don't you go and rebuke the devil, for God.*" I said, "Okay." I thought he had gotten tired, and needed some help at this point. So I with glee, was going to assist him. I didn't want him drained, and exhausted. So I got up and walked outside of my cottage door, and onto the back of the patio; to find the demons were out there as well. I also saw a device in the air; with beings on it, going up and down. I then spoke with authority; as much as I could muster at this point, "In the name of Jesus Christ of Nazareth, I rebuke you satan, you must leave." Now this resulted in nothing, absolutely nothing. Nothing left; no one left, it actually grew much worse - with many of them hissing at me. I went and sat down by God on the green; velvet futon, and wanted to deeply apologize to him, that my efforts were not successful, they didn't work – they were still there. *The demons were still there.*

God, very Fatherly and as a really concerned teacher spoke, "*Ann, the only way this is taken care of; is if you - Obey Me - then I will take care of this mess.*" "Obey?" I thought. I have never obeyed anyone, or tried to make that a priority in my life; whatsoever. I had never heard of this concept or system. But, this is the system; the only system. This is the absolute only way out; for all of us, period. It is like the law of gravity. This will never, ever change. If we obey; we reap Gods presence. If we do not obey; we are the unfortunate table scraps - for satan's brunch; both here upon this earth, and forevermore in eternity. We need to remember that satan, was on the earth first; before the human race. We need to remember he is still here; roaming to and fro, seeking anyone to devour;

1 PETER 5:8

"Be sober, Be vigilant; Because your adversary the devil,
As a roaring lion, Walketh about, Seeking whom he may devour."

♥

TWENTY EIGHT

THE WOODEN BENCH

The next thing I know – I was transported into a room, within the chambers of Hell. This room had a bench. This bench was long, wooden and hard. The bench had no back support or comfort; whatsoever. I was placed upon this bench, and could only sit or lie down. Demons were clawing at me, from every side and from every area; of that room. The room was totally canvassed with demons, in every shape and size imaginable. Demons are cursed by God. Demons are the ones that followed Lucifer in his rebellion, against God. Some live in Hell, some live in people and others roam the earth. Their heads are deformed, and they have faces like maggots. They are most ugly and hungry, to devour the people; who will not quit recreating, fellowshipping and sinning with them. They kept shouting at me, "*You think your Eve; You think your Eve.*"

There were two doors I kept looking at while there, one door to my right and one door straight ahead of me. I knew once you crossed through those doors, there would be no way out, there would be; no way of escape. I knew the judgment could not be altered, once you were inside and through those doors. I knew through those doors, was a very suffocating heat - that would nearly strangle, any living being. I could somewhat feel that heat and sensation, while sitting upon the bench. I looked at these demons trying to claw me. They were full of deep, raw hatred. They lost their opportunity to be with God, for all eternity. They longed for me to lose mine. This is their nature, this is their desire, this is their hope, and this is their drive.

They are very jealous, and bitter beings of mankind; for we have an opportunity; for eternal life. I was growing very tired and fatigued, on this bench. I was so afraid to close my eyes, as I felt I would fall off the bench; and into one of their deformed, grotesque arms. I knew they would devour me, if this happened. So I was forcing myself to stay very alert, and wide awake. Time went on, and on and on. I had no idea of how long I was there, as I had no sense of time. I wasn't sure, if I would ever get out of this place. I thought that I might be stuck there forever, and what a horrible - sickening feeling this was. No bad day on earth, compares with this. I was desperate for God to come, and rescue me out of this place. Then he finally showed up – to my deep, and utter gratefulness.

All of a sudden, I saw to my left; these glass stairs - that began to unfold, out of the air and down onto the ground; somewhat like an escalator would roll. These glass stairs - had light beaming from within, the very center of them. The glass stairs resembled big chunks of ice. I then saw the legs of Almighty God, coming down those stairs. Once again his legs look like pillars; clear, strong, thick pillars. Light was beaming through, and from them. I was so relieved to see him, but I couldn't move – much less cry. I felt like I was frozen on this bench; forever. Then God spoke, "*If you are not going to be "Holy," this is what you get; and I am leaving you.*"

HEBREWS 12:14

"Follow peace with all men, and holiness,
Without which no man shall see the Lord."

Please refer to - *Important Scriptures*, at the end of this book; on this most vital issue.

God then turned around, and walked right back up those steps. I then screamed bloody murder for him, as I was completely terrorized to my bones; and he took me right out. Then all; completely *vanished*. I then found myself back inside of; *The Natural Seen Realm*; of life; consisting of solid flesh, material and substance.

I was very concerned about immediately learning, what *Holiness* was; for I never wanted to return, to that location again. This was a very serious, and life threatening situation. God had given me a warning, and a commandment; in order for me not to be thrown into; *"The Lake of Fire,"* with the rebellious. I had absolutely no *"Fear of God"* before this episode; whatsoever. I didn't understand the scripture, about the *"Fear of God,"* or the need to *"Fear the Lord."* God was; in my mind - just, *"A Good Ole God,"* who loved us, no matter what we did. Well he does love us; but when we die, if we do not live right; we absolutely do, go straight to Hell. This is not a myth, but a complete factual account; of truth.

God told me that he cannot change his book, for any of us. Life has been written, and cannot be altered. We must change, in order to live in Heaven. God will help us, every step of the way. You can count on that. God has standards and commands; and we must learn to submit, love, embrace and follow them; on a daily basis. God loves you and he is calling every one of you, at this very moment in time to - *Choose Life*;

PROVERBS 9:10

"The Fear of the LORD is, the beginning of Wisdom:
And the Knowledge of the Holy is, Understanding."

If we do not listen, learn and obey here; we will all end up in Hell later; period. You do not want to end up there. God does not want you there; either. Let us be *Holy*, as God is *Holy*.

TWENTY NINE

THE RIVER RIDE

I was back in my cottage, pondering all of the events that had transpired in my life. All of a sudden, the presence of the Lord appeared. I could see into the invisible realm once again. I witnessed the same pack of demons; that had been inside of my cottage, as before. "How do I get rid of these things?" I wondered. "When do they leave?" This was becoming pure, utter madness. I could see the demons, and sense the presence of the angels. The Lord kept telling me, "*Go to the Cross! Go to the Cross!*" I was tired and frantic, for this to finally be over; once and for all. I finally asked, "Where is the Cross?" The angels then began pointing for me to run, in a certain direction.

The direction they were suggesting, would take me right outside of my cottage's back door. I was not in the mood, for all of this adventure; at this time; in the wee hours of the morning. But God wasn't watching, any clock. It was all so frantic and serious. I felt like I was in a fight, for my very soul and existence. I ended up running out the back door, with a heart full of fear and anxiety. I took off running around the cottage, and ended up on a path, in the back yard.

One angel then pointed for me to run off my deck, and right into the water. I was wondering why the angel would want me in the Caloosahatchee River, at 3:00 AM. I was completely tired, exhausted and drained. I frantically obliged; quickly running down the long wooden deck, from the cottage; and diving right into the mud packed, sea weed infested - dark river waters. I began swimming, at an alarming rate. I was shocked at that, as I had not exercised for years. I couldn't figure out where all this strength, and energy was coming from. I was fully clothed, and the wet material was getting heavy upon my body. I had on a beautiful green blouse, and golden pants. I am so grateful my clothing was of a light weight material, and not some heavy velvet sweat suit, or a pair of jeans for that matter; it might have induced drowning at that point.

I could see the angel's right beside me, in the middle of the water. Their presence was helping me to swim, and keep going. I than saw God, coming from behind, out of nowhere. He had on his usual dignified clothing, and white gloves to match. He was perched very astutely, upon his special river driving device. He was in charge; screaming, "*Get to the Cross, Get to the Cross!*" He was continually directing the goal, over all of the commotion; with his hand pointing, in a forward direction. I kept going on after that. I was doing strokes; at a very athletic pace, but I was getting tired. Then all of a sudden, a beautiful, bright blue, diamond encrusted chariot; flew down, right out of the midnight sky.

On this device was non-other than our Lord, Savior and Creator; Jesus, The Christ - The Risen Messiah, and the King of Israel. He was beaming from ear to ear. He was shouting with great glee, at the top of his lungs, "*Go Annie Go, Go Annie Go!*" He called me, "*Annie.*" That touched me deeply. He knows our names, every single one of us. He looked great. He looked alive. He looked exuberant. He looked full of life. He looked very, very happy. He looked able. He looked completely full of energy, and filled with total enthusiasm; for he is – *Enthusiasm*.

He was wearing a blue diamond, encrusted suit; that was very, very nice. His smile was bigger, than the moon. His teeth are brilliant, shiny and pure white. He was full, of absolute joy. He is joy. He kept cheering me onward; as he would throw balls down to me; from his dazzling, blue diamond; encrusted chariot. These balls were made of the colors; red, white and blue; the colors of the American flag. These colors were full of light, and they sparkled beautifully; in the night sky. God loves America, and all the other nations; in which he alone has made. God longs to be understood and followed; by all of creations inhabitants. God longs, to protect us. Creation is the work of God's hands, and his hands alone.

I was trying to catch the balls, the Lord was throwing me; from his blue chariot. They were of a substance, very similar to bubbles; the kind you blow and find in your bubble bath. I tried taking the Lords hand, when he would swoop down real low; to cheer me on - but he would fly off again; very quickly. They are both extremely quick, him and God.

I continued swimming in the river, and looking for the Cross they wanted me to go to. Jesus was giving me energy, and so were the angels. I would become sad at the loss of not being taken by Christ, as he would reach down very close to me. I thought he would grab me at any moment; and pull me inside of his flying chariot. But, he only continued to press me forward; shouting loudly, and extremely animated, "*Go to the Cross! Go to the Cross*! Jesus Christ was my *Evangelist*. The Greek word for *evangelist* is *euaggelistēs,* which means; a bringer of good tidings.

When I felt myself getting tired and weary; I would find God close behind me, in his water chariot; as I have grown accustomed to calling it. He displayed a very stern and determined demeanor upon his face, and this kept me going, "*To the Cross*!" He would shout and point, "*Get rid of the black underwear!*" He was shouting this over and over. He wanted me to repent, of the adultery I was in. Adultery is a sin. If this sin is not repented of; meaning stopped, the person participating in this sin; will enter into eternal damnation, if they die - in this sin;

1 CORINTHIANS 6:9-10

"Know ye not that the unrighteous shall not inherit the Kingdom of God? Be not deceived: neither fornicators, nor idolaters, nor adulterers, nor effeminate, nor abusers of themselves with mankind. ¹⁰ Nor thieves, nor covetous, nor drunkards, nor revilers, nor extortioners, shall inherit the Kingdom of God."

I was swimming as fast as I could. I could feel my body becoming completely full of exhaustion. I felt like I was nearly close to collapsing; and then God would continue to shout, "*Get rid of those black underwear!*" I looked into my golden pants, and found to my shock; that

I was wearing black underwear. I reached in and ripped the black underwear; from my body. I then threw them at God. He settled down at that point, about the black underwear. He didn't want me possessed with sin anymore. He didn't want me; in *The Lake of Fire*. He was cutting the sexual immoral acts from me, for good. God is always trying to save us. This is pure, genuine, and true; *perfect love*, at its finest. *Thank you, God.*

He continued to direct me forward and onto, "The Cross." He also showed me Lucifer. Lucifer was walking in the water, toward me. God spoke, *"You can go with him, your rights and the world, and then onto Hell; or you can go to, "The Cross" with me and "The Bible." That's it! Those are your choices in life, the only two that are."*

I was desperate to locate a Cross somewhere. I had been swimming in the dark, muddy, sea-weedy Caloosahatchee River; in the middle of the wee hours of the morning, for hours it seemed. I was having a hard time locating a *"Cross"* of any kind, alongside the river bank; in the dark of the night. Jesus Christ kept swooping down close to me; cheering me on and sending loads of energy into me - so I could make it. So I wouldn't die; so I could breathe, and move my limbs even further along,

PSALM 18:9-10

"He bowed the heavens also, and came down: And darkness was under his feet. [10] And he rode upon a cherub, and did fly: Yea, He did fly upon the wings of the wind."

♥

After being in the water awhile, I became extremely concerned of how far I had actually swam down, from my cottage dock. I didn't have my contacts in, and my vision wasn't good. But I kept on swimming, as my options were very limited at this point; to say the least. I was frantic to find, a "*Cross!*" I kept seeing the devil, walking in the water toward me, I knew that I would be safe; once I reached a "*Cross.*" I kept eyeballing God on his special water device, and the astute gentlemen that sat so upright; right next to him. I never saw anyone like this person, in my life. Clean, perfect and excellent describe him best. His name; is "The Holy Spirit." He was dressed like a "Founding Father of America."

To my delight, a bright "*Cross*" finally appeared upon the river bank. It was all lit up, so that I could see it. I swam even harder to the side of the river, to exit and to crawl up the bank; to get near this "*Cross.*" My heart was beating fast, as Lucifer was right behind me.

I climbed up and over, these sharp pointed rocks. I could feel my feet getting cut, and blood beginning to ooze from my wounds. But, I pressed on and made it up that hill. I ran over to the "*Cross,*" and touched it, for that is all I knew to do at the "*Cross.*" I could see that the area, was filled with angels. These angels looked pretty peaceful. They were just standing there present with me, looking on. I stood there at the "*Cross*" awhile, and wondered how I would ever make it back to the cottage. I didn't know where I was. I only knew that I was soaking wet, and without my contacts or glasses to see.

All of a sudden, the Lord descended in his blue chariot; in the middle of a driveway, to the front of the river. He began leading me back home. I just knew to follow his prompting, as he would come close; and then take off in a certain direction, within the air. I noticed he had the road all lit up, with beautiful angels. They were all blue in color. They were standing at his attention, for this wayward, lost child of his. I just kept looking at these angels, as they outlined the roadside for me. I was extremely fatigued, dripping wet and somewhat mad, to say the least. I was thrilled for their help, but sad to be left here upon the earth; instead of going home with him. I finally arrived at the cottage. I took a long hot shower, and wrapped my head within a towel. I then fell into a deep, needed sleep; to my utter surprise and extreme gratefulness.

The next day, God was there at the cottage. He knew I was severely disappointed; in *"The trip that did not last."* So he spoke, *"Okay, we are going to Heaven today. I hope you are ready to leave "Tex" and the kids."* I felt very sad inside, at the thought of that; but I didn't want to hurt God's feelings. So I with a stiff upper lip said, *"Okay – time to go!"* So the place turned into a Heavenly airplane, and off we went. The angle of the cottage room had changed into a takeoff mode, pointing upward into the sky.

The Lord is magnetic. You just long to be with him. This is his personality. But a deep sense of loss, began to grow within my heart. I loved my husband and my children, and I longed to be with them. I know the Lord was not hurt at this; for this was his work, for he creates hearts; and he had created mine.

The trip to Heaven was taking so long. I began to squirm after awhile. We were all flying upward, but making little, if any progress. I began to really ponder my family at this point. I said to him, "No Lord, I want to go home." Then God began to speak with me about going home, and what lie ahead.

THIRTY

THE OTHER WOMAN

I was alarmed at the movie that began to play; right in front, of my very own two eyes. Starring in this movie, was none other than "Tex" himself; with another woman. Both of them were completely, and totally nude; doing sexual exploits with one another. I gazed at this screen, and then the screen vanished quickly – but the truth was revealed. What else would God reveal, but the truth? God is absolute; truth. God spoke, *"Tex" is with her, and I need your help in getting him out; of satan's hands."* I told God "This cannot possibly be true. "Tex" would never do anything like this." God didn't say another word. I promised God that I would pack up, and go home. But I went to my sisters instead; to cozy in. God came with me. I felt like I was dragging around a dead corpse, and that dead corpse was me. God knew my condition, and he knew "Tex's" condition.

God knew "Tex's" attitude. God heard the conversations we had spoken together, in person and by phone. God even heard the conversations when we were "*Alone*." There is no hiding from God. God heard "Tex's" word's to me; flowing from a mouth of pride and vanity, as he continually pushed me aside with the, "*Get Lost*" messages; coming from his lips. God knew everything "Tex" was doing. I did not. God wanted "Tex" safe, from the things; he knew nothing of.

While cozying in at my sisters, I saw some pretty grotesque demons present. These demons are allowed entry into ones dwelling, if there is sin in your life. You may not see them, but I guarantee you; they are present. I had been sitting out on my sister's lanai, and witnessed some very sickening things. There was a demon riding upon a mule, with *dirty oil* all over it. He came riding up close to me, trying to brush up against me; in a sexual manner. He was licking his lips, and making sickening noises. I was deeply horrified, to my core. I screamed at the demon, and then it *vanished*.

THIRTY ONE

THE SATELLITE DISH

I then saw another demon, standing at a distance across the apartment complex. He was smoking a pipe, with a straw hat upon his head. He was standing beside a satellite dish; pressing down upon the lever, of the satellite dish. Black smoke began to fill the atmosphere in the sky, as he did this. This devil was in charge of the "*Media and Television Ministry*," of satan's here, upon the earth. The devil is in charge of polluting the hearts, and lives of all people; underneath the sun. God spoke, "*The devil has polluted my earth.*" satan has many weapons he uses against us, on earth. This is one of them. He creates the "*Media.*" He creates; his entertainment. He creates; his deception. We the creation, watch his "*Media,*" that is completely full - and laced with sin. We then become polluted and corrupted; by what we watch. God wants all people; to stop fellowshipping with satan, through all his "*Media*" sources;

PROVERBS 19:27

"Cease, my son, to hear the instruction that causeth to err, from the words of knowledge."

People then commit the sins; they have just viewed, to their, *"Destruction and Loss."* This is a widely - successful method that satan uses, to gain entry into not only our homes; but our bodies and minds as well. This form of deception, has destroyed many lives here upon the earth. Many souls are in the chambers of Hell - as a result. God does not want anyone drinking out of the devils toilets, and experiencing *death* as a result. *Death to the mind, body, soul, spirit, families, communities and nations.* We are all commanded to come out; and be separate;

MATTHEW 6:23

"But if thine eye be evil, thy whole body shall be full of darkness. If therefore the light that is in thee be darkness, how great is that darkness!"

When you invite the devil in, you get the reward - of *Death*;

JOHN 10:10

"The thief cometh not, but for to steal, and to kill, and to destroy: I am come that they might have life, and that they might have it more abundantly."

Please choose Christ and reap the reward - of *Life*.

THIRTY TWO

THE HAIRY BEAST

I noticed a dark hairy beast, standing in the corner of the living room; at my sister's apartment. This being was very large. This being was full of evil, and darkness. I lit up a cigarette, and all Hell broke loose. I began to scream and heard God say, "*Well, what do you want me to do; with him? Where would you like for me, to take this beast?*" In other words, "*You invited him here - through your sin; now you want me to take him? Why not get rid of the sin that invites him in - to park within your life instead?*" God was trying to remind me, of the former teaching. *I obey, he takes the devils away. I do not obey, the devils get to stay. See the insanity trap. See the war? See the reason; to obey?*

The devil lives, where he is invited. Well, I wanted my cake (cigarette); and I wanted to eat (smoke) it too. I wanted to smoke, without the demonic guests; that come along with it. God very clearly told me, "*No Smoking.*" I wish I would have listened to him then. I fell asleep that night, seeing Jesus Christ standing right beside me. I do not believe, I have ever slept this good, in my life. *Thank You Lord.*

THIRTY THREE

PONDERING HOME

The next morning I awoke, and examined all the cuts and bruises; that were inflicted upon my feet, from the rock climbing "*Cross*" episode. There were quite a few to say the least. I began to think about my life. "*Home*" was very heavy, upon my heart. I didn't know how to get back in. I was very despondent. My sister had invited a friend over from Miami, to hopefully cheer me up. This visitor only dragged me down further. This friend had nothing good to say whatsoever, for he didn't know God. He only gave carnal, worldly advice; which leads to hopelessness, which leads to death – *the death of faith*; which leads to suicidal thoughts. He didn't have or possess truth, so – he could not give it. You cannot give; what you do not own.

I then decided to rent another place along the river, due to the fact I couldn't move back home. I would go over to this cute, small house many times and just sit alongside the riverbank. I was waiting for the owners to vacate, so I could then move in. I saw God standing in the water, on one occasion. He was pointing his thumb down; like this was a *"No Go."* I got the message. The message was; *"Wrong Way."* So I knew that plan wasn't going to work. But how was I ever, to get back home?

Did you realize that God loves, to direct our path? Please read this scripture and smile. You are not meant to lead, your own way. God will do that for you, and peace will follow;

PROVERBS 3:5-6

"Trust in the LORD with all thine heart; and lean not unto thine own understanding. ⁶ In all thy ways acknowledge him, and he shall direct thy paths."

I went back to my sister's for the night. Upon lying down for the evening, the patriarchs surrounded me. They were smiling broadly; encouraging me *"To Press On."* They looked of great age, but had no wrinkles. Their hair was thick, healthy and very white in color. They had big barreled chests, and nice clothing on too. It was so nice and refreshing to see them. I know one of them was *Moses*. They told me so. God allows us to see the others, to encourage us;

MATTHEW 17:1-3

"And after six days Jesus taketh Peter, James, and John his brother, and bringeth them up into an high mountain apart, ² And was transfigured before them: and his face did shine as the sun, and his raiment was white as the light. ³ And, behold, there appeared unto them Moses and Elias talking with him."

♥

God was encouraging me, to not give up. God was encouraging me; to believe in him. I heard God speak, "*It is time to pack it up, move out and plan on going home*." I could not understand God's insistence on this issue; due to the fact, I wasn't wanted at home. But God was very emphatic, about his desire for me to be there. He wanted me to stand my ground, take back the children and raise them. He wanted me to pursue a relationship, with my husband. For God is *"The Word,"* and the scripture clearly tell us;

1 CORINTHIANS 7:16

"For what knowest thou, O wife, whether thou shalt save thy husband? Or how knowest thou, O man, whether thou shalt save thy wife?"

♥

God wanted me to take back my position, at our business. He wanted me to be a good help mate, and a *"Proverbs 31"* wife to "Tex," I had always tried to be; for this is the correct, Biblical protocol. I was wronged. But I had been doing wrong; so we needed to clear the deck, and begin again. *"Was it really possible?"* I wondered. I was pondering God's words over and over in my mind. I went back to the cottage, for a few nights. I thought it would be pretty nice, to have a few *"last evening's"* there. The place was very special to me. I spent so much time there, with the Lord; learning from his heart about how to *live, and why*.

THIRTY FOUR

THE RAPTURE

One night, back at the tiny little cottage, the Lord arrived and showed me "*The Rapture*." I saw many spirits, all arrayed in bright white. They were leaning over the balconies in Heaven. They were really excited, about what God was going to do. God showed me how he was going to open up the graves, and out would fly everyone's bodies. They would then rise up into the sky, and be attached to their spirit. You could tell; God was excited about this;

1 THESSALONIANS 4:16-17

"For the Lord himself shall descend from heaven with a shout, with the voice of the archangel, and with the trump of God: and the dead in Christ shall rise first: ¹⁷ Then we which are alive and remain shall be caught up together with them in the clouds, to meet the Lord in the air: and so shall we ever be with the Lord."

♥

THIRTY FIVE

THE AUDITORIUM

The next evening, I found myself in a beautiful auditorium; within Heaven. This place was decked out, and extremely elegant in every single way. The location was lined with dark red maroon, velvet drapes. These drapers were hanging from a very tall ceiling; and cascading down, barely touching the ground. There were a variety, of different golden tones present as well. Very exquisite God is. God is very affluent. God is very wealthy. God is very sophisticated. God has superb taste. Royalty; is the name for it;

1 PETER 2:9

"But ye are a chosen generation, a royal priesthood, an holy nation, a peculiar people; that ye should shew forth the praises of him, who hath called you out of darkness into his marvellous light."

The auditorium was packed, full of people when I arrived. The angels of the Lord were encamped around the interior, of the door entrances. Upon arriving into this palatial property, I looked down upon my dirty, stained clothing that I was wearing at the time. I felt so out of place. Everyone without exception was clean, bright, shiny, and beautiful. They were very well dressed, and put together. My hair was a hideous mess, and I didn't have a drop of makeup on. I turned to run out of this location, as I felt very awkward in being there. But God was faster than I, and caught me before I made the exit;

2 PETER 1:11

"For so an entrance shall be ministered unto you abundantly into The everlasting Kingdom of our Lord and Saviour, Jesus Christ."

God is very feisty and fast. He was all dressed up in dignified, fine clothing. He had on a shirt, which was buttoned up to his neck collar. The shirt was long sleeves. He had on a matching pair of pants. God's clothing fabric was very nice. He was in the colors of red and white stripes; very similar to the American flag. He had on pure white gloves to match. God is extremely strong, very masculine in appearance and very kind. He had on a beautiful, one of a kind pair of shoes, which were squarish at the toe. They were also red and white striped. He had on a belt as well.

I remember looking deep within his eyes in this auditorium, as I stood before him - in all of my filth. I never experienced such love and acceptance, in my life. He was utterly and amazingly kind, and generous to me. I could see *the centuries* in his face, as I stared into his. God's face, looks like rushing waters. I could also see his *deep concern* and *monumental anguish*, for his creation.

This concern of his, nearly killed my heart with pain. I could feel and sense his urgency to inform his creation; of reality, so that creation would live and not die. So all would know; *The absolute truth of life* – in order to, avoid satan and his future, at all costs. He wanted me to know the truth, and to choose eternal life; instead of eternal damnation. This is the heartbeat of *Our Heavenly Father*. His heart beats for you to live, and not to burn eternally, alongside the rebellious followers of satan here; which end up to all's sorrow, in the Lake of; non-ending Fire. He was transmitting these realities into my being in his way, which is *supernatural*; for our God is *supernatural*. I had always talked to God before, but never face to face. I was beaming with delight at being in his presence. I was consumed entirely with his deep concern, for his creation. The concern of amazing love; due to truth. He motioned for me to come in the auditorium, and have a seat;

EPHESIANS 2:1-6

"And you hath he quickened, who were dead in trespasses and sins; ² Wherein in time past ye walked according to the course of this world, according to the prince of the power of the air, the spirit that now worketh in the children of disobedience: ³ Among whom also we all had our conversation in times past, in the lusts of our flesh, fulfilling the desires of the flesh and of the mind; and were by nature the children of wrath, even as others. 4 But God, who is rich in mercy, for his great love wherewith he loved us. 5 Even when we were dead in sins, hath quickened us together with Christ, (by grace ye are saved;) 6 And hath raised us up together, and made us sit together in heavenly places in Christ Jesus."

God's kindness deeply overwhelmed, and floored me. I felt very shy and unworthy to be there. It was so outlandishly elegant, in every single way. I tried to leave once again – but, he wouldn't have it. I literally felt like I was in a dream come true. He pointed to me with those hands of his; all decked out in white gloves, to follow him inside - down the long, auditorium walkway. He kept saying, "*It's okay, It's okay.*" So I went in behind him. He motioned for me to sit down, on a chair ledge in the aisle. So I sat down and he took the seat in front of me, on the ledge of his chair;

DANIEL 7:9

"The Ancient of Days Did Sit."

I just sat there grinning at him, from ear to ear. I didn't quite know what to do, as God had never taken me to Heaven before. He was just always with me at work it seemed. My legs must have been wide open, as I was sitting on the ledge of this chair - because he, all at once motioned for me to cross my legs. I did, and then he crossed his as well. He wants us to be lady like here, for he created us; for that purpose. I knew this place was packed. I could just feel it. But I was too shy, to look around the room. So I just stared at him instead. He looked to the side, and I stared at his profile. He has quite a thick barreled chest, and a thick - strong neck as well. I examined him to the tee. He then whistled, and looked around the room – as I continued to stare at him; *in awe*. The love I felt for him, was overwhelming. He is kind. *He is Our Father;*

MATTHEW 6:9

"Our Father which art in Heaven, Hallowed be thy name."

God is Our Father, the one who created each; and every single one of us. He is so humble, for who he is. As we sat there, he gazed around the room, and continued to whistle. I noticed every single thing about him. His ears, his nose, his eyes, his neck, his legs, his arms, his chest and his heart. He then motioned for me to look in a certain direction, across the room. I did not. I continued to stare at him instead. Finally with a huge, big grin upon his face, he looked at me and said, "*Look!*" I then looked and saw Mom, sitting in the auditorium. She was totally alive, all bright, beautiful and thrilled. I know she was happy to see me. I started to cry; with joy. There are no words that can truly describe, the feelings you experience; when you see someone that was dead, that you loved with all of your heart and soul – now alive, and full of every wonderful thing imaginable. Joy unspeakable and full of absolute Glory, might describe it best;

PSALM 16:11

"Thou wilt shew me the path of life:
In thy presence is fullness of joy;
At thy right hand, there are pleasures forevermore."

They are all waiting for us in Heaven. God is waiting for you. His love for you fills my heart, many hours of my days; and now many years. His love for you makes me weep, and run for your souls.

God motioned to me, with his white gloves. He then pointed to the stage, in the auditorium. I believe he was saying that he has plans for me, to share my experience with you; his beloved creation. You are the object of his greatest love, and desire. You truly are. He has plans for each, and every single one of you. He longs to be your *Dad*. He longs to be your *Father*. He longs to be your *God*.

The Lord Jesus Christ shows us the Father, and then he turns our hearts toward Him;

MATTHEW 11:27

"All things are delivered unto me of my Father: and no man knoweth the Son, but the Father; neither knoweth any man the Father, save the Son, and he to whomsoever the Son will reveal Him."

When the Lord appears to people, he has great plans to bring truth, freedom, life and deliverance, unto them and to creation;

GENESIS 12:7

"And the LORD appeared unto Abram, and said, Unto thy seed will I Give This land: and there builded he an altar unto the LORD, Who appeared unto him."

♥

GENESIS 17:1-4

"And when Abram was ninety years old and nine, the LORD appeared to Abram, and said unto him, I am the Almighty God; walk before me, and be thou perfect. ² And I will make my covenant between me and thee, and will multiply thee exceedingly. ³ And Abram fell on his face: and God talked with him, saying, ⁴As for me, behold, my covenant is with thee, and thou shalt be a father of many Nations."

♥

GENESIS 18:1

"And the LORD appeared unto him in the plains of Mamre: And he sat in the tent door in the heat of the day."

♥

GENESIS 26:1-2

"And there was a famine in the land, beside the first famine that was in the days of Abraham. And Isaac went unto Abimelech king of the

Philistines unto Gerar. ² And the LORD appeared unto him, and Said, Go not down into Egypt; dwell in the land which I shall tell thee of."

God continues to appear, to give clarity and direction;

GENESIS 26:24

"And the LORD appeared unto him the same night, and said, I am the God of Abraham thy father: fear not, for I am with thee, and will bless thee, and multiply thy seed for my servant Abraham's sake."

God continues to appear – so that people will press on, to complete their destiny;

GENESIS 32:22-30

"And he rose up that night, and took his two wives, and his two women servants, and his eleven sons, and passed over the ford Jabbok. ²³ And he took them, and sent them over the brook, and sent over that he had. ²⁴ And Jacob was left alone; and there wrestled a man with him until the breaking of the day. ²⁵ And when he saw that he prevailed not against him, he touched the hollow of his thigh; and the hollow of Jacob's thigh was out of joint, as he wrestled with him. ²⁶ And he said, Let me go, for the day breaketh. And he said, I will not let thee go, except thou bless me. ²⁷ And he said unto him, What is thy name? And he said, Jacob. ²⁸And he said, Thy name shall be called no more Jacob, but Israel: for as a prince hast thou power with God and with men, and hast prevailed.

²⁹And Jacob asked him, and said, Tell me, I pray thee, thy name. And he said, Wherefore is it that thou dost ask after my name? And he blessed him there. ³⁰ And Jacob called the name of the place Peniel: for I have seen God face to face, and my life is preserved."

Exodus 3:16

"Go, and gather the elders of Israel together, and say unto them, The LORD God of your fathers, the God of Abraham, of Isaac, and of Jacob, appeared unto me, saying, I have surely visited you, and seen that which is done to you in Egypt."

You are never alone, God sees all;

EXODUS 16:10

"And it came to pass, as Aaron spake unto the whole congregation of the children of Israel, that they looked toward the wilderness, and, behold, the glory of the LORD appeared in the cloud."

EXODUS 24:10-11

"And they saw the God of Israel: and there was under his feet as it were a paved work of a sapphire stone, and as it were the body of heaven in his clearness. [11] And upon the nobles of the children of Israel, he laid not his hand: also they saw God, and did eat and drink."

EXODUS 33:11

"And the LORD spake unto Moses face to face, as a man speaketh unto his friend. And he turned again into the camp: but his servant Joshua, the son of Nun, a young man, departed not out of the tabernacle."

LEVITICUS 9:23

"And Moses and Aaron went into the tabernacle of the congregation, and came out, and blessed the people: and the glory of the LORD appeared unto all the people."

NUMBERS 14:10

"But all the congregation bade stone them with stones. And the glory of the LORD appeared in the Tabernacle of the congregation before all the children of Israel."

NUMBERS 16:19

"And Korah gathered all the congregation against them unto the door of the tabernacle of the Congregation: and the glory of the LORD appeared unto all the congregation."

NUMBERS 16:42

"And it came to pass, when the congregation was gathered against Moses and against Aaron, that they looked toward the tabernacle of the congregation: and, behold, the cloud covered it, and the glory of the LORD appeared."

NUMBERS 20:6

"And Moses and Aaron went from the presence of the assembly unto the door of the tabernacle of the Congregation, and they fell upon their faces: and the glory of the LORD appeared unto them."

DEUTERONOMY 5:1-4

"And Moses called all Israel, and said unto them, Hear, O Israel, the statutes and judgments which I speak in your ears this day, that ye may learn them, and keep, and do them. ² The LORD our God made a covenant with us in Horeb. ³ The LORD made not this covenant with our fathers, but with us, even us, who are all of us here alive this day. ⁴ The LORD talked with you face to face in the mount out of the midst of the fire."

DEUTERONOMY 31:15

"And the LORD appeared in the tabernacle in a pillar of a cloud: and the pillar of the cloud stood over the door of the tabernacle."

1 SAMUEL 3:21

"And the LORD appeared again in Shiloh: for the LORD revealed himself to Samuel in Shiloh, by the word of the LORD."

1 KINGS 3:5

"In Gibeon the LORD appeared to Solomon in a dream by night: and God said, ask what I shall give thee."

1 KING 9:1-2

"And it came to pass, when Solomon had finished the building of the house of the LORD, and the king's house, and all Solomon's desire which he was pleased to do, ² That the LORD appeared to Solomon the second time, as he had appeared unto him at Gibeon."

1 KINGS 11:9

"And the LORD was angry with Solomon, because his heart was turned from the LORD God of Israel, which had appeared unto him twice."

2 CHRONICLES 3:1

"Then Solomon began to build the house of the LORD at Jerusalem in mount Moriah, where the Lord appeared unto David his father, in the place that David had prepared in the threshing floor of Ornan The Jebusite."

2 CHRONICLES 7:12

"And the LORD appeared to Solomon by night, and said unto him, I have heard thy prayer, and have chosen this place to myself for an house of sacrifice."

ACTS 7:55-56

"But he, being full of the Holy Ghost, Looked up stedfastly into heaven, and saw the glory of God, and Jesus standing on the right hand of God, 56 And said, behold, I see the heavens opened, and the Son of Man standing on the right hand of God."

As we know the Bible clearly tells us, when Jesus was on the earth; God was not seen – as recorded in these scriptures;

JOHN 1:18

"No man hath seen God at any time, the only begotten Son, which is in the bosom of the Father, he hath declared him."

1 JOHN 4:12

"No man hath seen God at any time."

Since the tabernacle veil was torn; which was Jesus flesh, his blood now covers us. We now have full access, to the Father. We also know that it is Jesus, who shows us the Father;

1 TIMOTHY 6:13-15

"I give thee charge in the sight of God, who quickeneth all things and before Christ Jesus, who before Pontius Pilate witnessed a good confession; 14 That thou keep this commandment without spot, unrebukable, until the appearing of our Lord Jesus Christ: 15 Which in his times he shall shew, who is the blessed and only Potentate, The King of kings, and Lord of lords."

♥

THIRTY SIX

GOD'S PLAN FOR YOU

I hope you have enjoyed my story, about *Our God*; the one and only "*Creator of the Universe.*" I hope you find hope, in him alone. He is real and he is all you will ever need, for he alone possesses - all that is.

I pray you will seek him for yourself, and come into an eternal, daily relationship with him; allowing him to teach and to keep you, under his safety. For this alone; is his supreme desire.

I hope you live each day to the fullest, with an eye on your eternity, and your fellowman, knowing that to obey Jesus Christ - *is the key to life, and the entrance into eternal life*.

HEBREWS 5:9

"Being made perfect, he became the author of eternal salvation unto all them that *obey him*."

♥

We are here to learn, and to become God's children; in total purity, devotion, understanding, surrender, submission, love, respect, fellowship, obedience and service.

THIRTY SEVEN

THE REPORT

I wish I could report, that all of the huge efforts God and I put into my marriage; turned out great. But they did not. My husband left the path of life, and our marriage. But God has been re-building me, ever since. I am very thankful to him; for his continual, steadfast, loving presence and faithfulness to me. There is no one like; *Our Great God*, absolutely no one.

I am also thrilled to report, that my body has been pain free; ever since the glorious day, of my physical healing and deliverance. I have also grown much in my walk with God; in truth, understanding and love; for him and you - his beautiful creation.

If I would have *known* to take the vital and necessary time, to be grounded and taught; in the truth of life, "*The Holy Bible*," after my born again salvation experience, in my youth; I would have never experienced the heartaches, which are the result of people; who possess *lack of knowledge*. God clearly warns us, for our own good and wellbeing;

HOSEA 4:6

"My people are destroyed, for lack of knowledge."

Yes, I would have had afflictions and trials; like all of us. But I would have made my decisions; with the Lord leading and directing me; through his "Word - The Bible," through his "Spirit," and through his *"Peace,"* instead of running from bad situations - due to abuse, trauma, fear and *"No Way Outs."*

Becoming grounded, in the principles and doctrine of Christ; is mandatory, vital and essential; for a healthy, happy, whole and beautiful life. So please get settled, in a good Bible teaching Church; under the submission, love and concern of a Pastor; where you can grow, in the knowledge of God. This will benefit your life, as you get to know God; and as you allow him, to guide and direct your journey; based upon your knowledge, trust and faith in him; as the days and years go by. God can then make your life something pure, unique, meaningful and deeply beautiful.

It is amazing to me how God brings you all the way back; to the precise point, in your life – where *the mistake* was made. This is done to eradicate and discard the life - that was really, never meant to be. God destroys *the counterfeit, permissive will life*; and re-builds you and your life; the way he intended it to look, when he originally designed and created you. Do not be surprised, if this is where you find your journey at; or where it ends up - in the future. Hang on to God. His love for you; is completely good, perfect and sound. He knows what he is doing. Please trust him, no matter how deep the pain is, or how confusing it might be; at this point. Your life will unfold into something whole, and extremely beautiful. Please be patient with the process, God doesn't waste anything;

ROMANS 8:28

"And we know that all things work together for good to them that love God, to them who are the called according to his purpose."

I wish to extend an invitation to you, to enjoy a very special website experience - that has been developed with the Lord, especially for you. The name of the website is RealOron® – www.RealOron.org.

RealOron has been produced to help you grow, and to mature in; *The Knowledge of Life*. This has been created for your edification, strength, safety and health. This is a place designed to keep you, within the arms of eternal love and purity; *The Arms; of Almighty God*.

THIRTY EIGHT

TO THE ABUSED

Many walk our earth and planet, with huge gaping holes; deep within them. I know - I was one of them. The road out and up; is extremely agonizing, painful and hard. But you can do it; if you focus on the end result, and ignore a lot of annoying, painful, discouraging, horrific and frustrating things; along the way.

JEREMIAH 29:11 is one of the scripture promises, which God has given to all of us. Please hold onto this scripture, through your journey; on the earth;

JEREMIAH 29:11

"For I know the thoughts that I think toward you, saith the LORD,
Thoughts of peace, and not of evil,
To give you; an expected end."

♥

Here is the other important scripture, which goes with this;

GENESIS 18:18-19

"Seeing that Abraham shall surely become a great and mighty nation and all the nations of the earth shall be blessed in him. ¹⁹ For I know him, that he will command his children and his household after him and they shall keep the way of the LORD, to do justice and judgment; that the LORD may bring upon Abraham that which he hath spoken of him."

♥

Now, the combination of you doing your part, and knowing God will do his part; is *Unbeatable*. This relationship with God, and your expected end is based upon you; *following God's instructions*; regardless of any circumstance; that comes to you, or against you.

You must keep the way of the Lord. (*Do not let satan, or others stop you*.) Many refuse to do their part, and then forfeit their great expected end. Please do not abort your expected end, and destiny. If you have dropped out of the race, get back in. It is never, too late. God is waiting, ready and able.

The end will be manifested; and will most certainly come to pass, as you continue forward with the Lord. You must get going, with sheer determination and God; to make this long and sometimes painful journey; to wholeness, freedom and destiny.

Please be patient with yourself, others and God. Surrender to God's pace, timing and personal direction; for your life. Follow him, in spite of it all. Lean not, on your own understanding. Trust him, and the direction he gives you.

I promise you, you will make it, if you do not quit. It is like any goal. You write the goal. You write the process, and then you start knocking things off; one thing at a time, one day at a time, and one year at a time; until – you are there.

If you need to rest, please do so. Rest is a God thing. Remember God is working with you, every step of the way. Lean totally on him; and believe your great expected end - will come to pass.

You were *Born Again*; to get the *Victory* - and you will. Do not quit. Remember your *Dad is God*, and he is for you. Please celebrate your progress, along the way. Let's get started.

THIRTY NINE

MOVING FORWARD

- Always keep moving forward, with Christ.
- Separate yourself and your children from the abuser; for your safety and wellbeing. You were not born, to be a punching bag.
- Stay in *"The Way, The Truth & The Life"* with Jesus Christ, always and forever.
- Stay out of the trash cans of satan, that are here upon the earth, for they will surely destroy you.
- Seek Godly counsel from a born again, Holy Spirit filled person; that will counsel you; from *"The Word of God; The Bible."*
- Stay in church and continue to grow in Christ, allowing him to give you; *"Life More Abundantly."* (JOHN 10:10)
- Get up daily; brush and floss your teeth, groom, exercise and eat healthy.

- Take one step at a time, moving forward; in peace, purpose and patience; for yourself and others.
- Stay full of hope for your life; by reading the *Bible* day and night, for faith comes by hearing; "*The Word of God*."
- Don't be shy, talk to God.
- Stay full of joy by listening to good *Gospel* music and preaching, as well as *Gospel* programming and teaching.
- Have fellowship in *Bible Studies* and recreation, with people that live and walk with God here, upon the earth.
- Go to the lake, park or seaside, go for coffee, tea or ice cream, go through the thrift stores; giggle with joy and anticipation, of a better life; "*The Expected End*."
- Hold fast to God and the covenant promises, which he has given; to the ones who refuse to forsake him; knowing they will certainly and factually come to pass. (NUMBERS 23:19)
- Allow God to develop you, and your children's gifts.
- Allow God to re-arrange you, and your entire life.
- Be patient; with God.
- Allow God; to be the boss.
- Live in peace; remain calm and stable.
- Have faith in God; believe that he is honest, and will do what he has promised.
- Erect and maintain; healthy boundaries.

- Learn to say – "No."
- Don't overbook yourself.
- Don't let anyone; pressure you.
- Understand that you will always have critics, pray for them.
- Don't defend yourself; know who you are, and why.
- Continue in faith, holiness, patience, commitment and perseverance; never quit or give up.
- Get plenty of rest and remain in peace; no matter how big the storm screams.
- Get a massage, manicure or pedicure.
- Have a friend over; for lunch.
- Use Godliness and self-control.
- Try smoked almonds, and hot flavored peanuts.
- Feed the homeless; love, food and truth.
- Learn to value; yourself.
- Do a facial and apply a hair mask; weekly.
- Become concerned; about what concerns God.
- Straighten your closet, and give some good items to the poor.
- Enroll in God's team, and purpose.
- Allow God to teach you; manners.
- Look in the mirror and smile, at the creation that you are.

- Allow God to change your makeup, hairstyle and clothing.
- Ask for help, when you need it.
- Be the leader of your home. Rule with love, purpose, consistency and firmness; without apology.
- Take deep; long breaths.
- Smell lavender.
- Try wearing, different colors.
- Pray, for your relatives.
- Remember; *God is your Father*.
- Pray, for yourself.
- Encourage and Love; your Pastor.
- Desire the best for others, and use your gifts to help them make it.
- Compliment others.
- Learn not to worry, or to be anxious for anything. God is in charge and Jesus is Lord. They are overseeing personally; all of the details of your life. (MATTHEW 10:30)
- Do not be afraid of sacrifice, pain, suffering or living with less.
- Never worry, about what other people think. *Walk with God*.
- Enjoy watching, *Bible Movies*.
- Allow God to take you through the valleys and the wilderness, and then into; "*The Promised Land*," to remain.
- Enjoy the mountain tops; yours and others.

- Cry when you need to, and remember God is healing you; no matter what it looks like, how you feel, or how long it's been.
- Remember, you have done well and have come a long, long way. Applaud your progress.
- Let no one discourage, or dismantle you.
- Remember that God builds with small pieces; that turn into big stuff. Keep making.
- Remember, the angels love you.
- Be diligent, then enjoy rest.
- Don't let rejection stop, or hinder you.
- Be willing to let go of the people, who don't live or like; your way of life.
- Embrace humility, it is the fragrance of Jesus.
- Walk in obedience; it is the road of Christ.
- Embrace holiness; it is the person of God.
- Always set the joy before you; for this is Christ.
- Turn the other cheek, when people hurt you; then pray for them.
- Remember, your beginnings.
- Don't try to be understood, just obey God.
- Thank God, for your salvation.
- Pray for the repentance and salvation, of the nations.

- Be full of healthy self-esteem, and confidence in God. This is sanity, this is peace.
- Give to the under-dog, and help those in need; to have, to rise and to overcome.
- Remember God is making you; "*Holy and Royal.*"
- Spend some money; on yourself - without guilt.
- Try to drink; more water.
- Give away something, you love.
- Use your talents and time, to bless others.
- Expect good from God; this is hope.
- Trust God; even if it makes no sense. Always do as he says. For God is all good, and all wise.
- Remember that God knows what he is doing. He has been God, forever and always.
- Don't try to understand everything. Know that all things will, and do work together for good; to those who love God and are called; according to his purpose. (ROMANS 8:28)
- You will know the future; in the future.
- Believe the vision and walk in, and toward it. Do not waiver or doubt.
- Be quick to repent. Keep a clean heart, and pure hands; with God.
- Let no one steal or take away, your personal dream and destiny; which God has placed within you.

- If you get angry at God; *which you probably will*. Tell him, and then let it go; for his love for you is perfect. You will surely find this out; as he continues to propel you forward, minute after minute, hour after hour, day after day, week after week, month after month, year after year; until you are gone, from this earth. He wants only the best for you. *He is your Father.*
- Put on a good *Gospel* worship CD, at bedtime; or read a good *Gospel* book.
- Keep your home clean, tidy and organized.
- Go to the pet store, and love a puppy.
- Enjoy the wind.
- Begin to jog.
- Buy a goldfish.
- Clean your car.
- Enjoy God.
- Hug someone.
- Mow your grass.
- Weed your yard.
- Paint the mailbox.
- Iron your clothes.
- Enjoy the flowers.
- Drink orange juice.

- Try a Chai Tea Latte with honey, it's delicious.
- Learn to sew, crochet or paint.
- Make something unique, one of a kind and extremely beautiful.
- Go to the flea market.
- Teach the *Bible*.
- Do a puzzle.
- Paint a picture.
- Love others.
- Get involved in a *Ministry*, of some sort or the other; within your *Church*, or *Bible Study Group*.
- Play the *Audio Bible* while you are at home, sleeping or taking a nap.
- Make the world; beautiful.
- Make your dwelling; a sanctuary of God's love, presence, purpose, truth, holiness, consecration, joy and protection. (JOHN 14:23)
- Remember that you are God operated; meaning his Holy Spirit lives within you and he is your battery. You are not doing things entirely alone. You are a team; with God. (JOHN 1:12)
- Do not throw the towel in, for God is able; keep going.
- Allow God to propel you into your future, and divine destiny; under his able, steady direction and pace.
- Go for a walk.

- Wait for God's perfect will for your life, and refuse to settle for God's permissive will.
- Smell the daisies, and enjoy color.
- Rest; on the Sabbath.
- Transform an old desk.
- Remember, the angels are with you. (PSALM 91)
- Enjoy the small things, and keep things simple and light.
- Keep; a to do list. ·
- Light a candle, buy white towels and linens.
- Keep a calendar.
- Don't forget, to smile.
- Never say you're ugly, for God has fearfully and wonderfully; created you.
- Never say you can't; for you can do all things; through Christ; who strengthens you.
- Enjoy perfume, or cologne.
- Focus on the good, and forget the bad.
- Know that you were made and designed uniquely, by the Creator; for his pleasure, and purpose.
- Catch a butterfly, and then let it go.
- Enjoy a sunset.
- Know that the great cloud of witnesses - is cheering you on.

- Know that the Lord, *is for you.*
- Walk barefoot.
- Go for a bike ride.
- Remember that nothing is too hard, for the Lord. (GENESIS 18:14)
- Go to a Garage Sale.
- Know that the Lord wants you; to enjoy your life.
- Know that, your life really matters.
- Know that your life, has purpose and great importance.
- Remember, every single day; truly counts.
- Remember faith.
- Remember patience.
- Remember that God is always ready to forgive, just ask him to.
- Know that God deeply loves you, and he is making you; his *Masterpiece.* (GENESIS 1:26-28)

FOURTY

GOD'S AMAZING CHARACTER

The following detailed list describes what I noticed, about our Heavenly Father, Jesus Christ and the Holy Spirit; during the four months of being with them - *visually*. First and foremost, I discovered they are very special, in every single way. They are incredibly pure and tough as nails; in their protective battle against satan, and the destructive plans that the enemy has against our lives, both here and eternally. Here is his person;

- He can be mysterious.
- He causes us to ask, "What is he up to?"
- He is colorful, playful, interesting and overwhelming.
- He is our Savior.
- Jesus is his name, our Hero and our Champion.
- He is handsome, infallible and without limits.

- He is matchless, priceless, pure and true.
- He outstrips, outperforms, and outshines anything I have ever seen.
- He is elegant.
- He is stupendous, enormous and a mighty warrior.
- He is measureless, and has a great sense of humor.
- Merciful and forgiving; are his middle names.
- He is fun, dramatic and all together real.
- He is our Shepherd; The Creator of All Good Things.
- He is a historian, and he is futuristic.
- He is invisible.
- He is the Counselor, and Great Physician.
- He is a great friend, and a good companion.
- He is the driver, and calls us to come up higher; in our lives.
- He commands, "Let's go, you can do it."
- He believes in us, and is our greatest cheerleader.
- He loves us.
- He is witty, smart and majestic; in his manner.
- He is the Ruler, of God's Universe.
- He is The Lord, and all together captivating.
- He has wonderful "*Special Effects,*" when he arrives on the scene.
- He doesn't give up, and he refuses to take "No" for an answer.

- He is Sovereign and the Lamb of God, who took our sins away.
- He has an undivided heart, and is very set in his ways.
- He is compassionate, and extremely remarkable.
- He is the "King of kings," and "Lord of lords."
- He is eternal, he will never end.
- He is ever present, and highly recommended.
- We cannot live without him, for he gives each of us; all good things to enjoy.
- He is; Paradise on Earth.
- He is; *Our Heavenly Father*.
- Sophisticated describes him; very well.
- He is surprising, and highly intelligent.
- He is jealous, wanting only to love and protect us; from satan.
- He loves to spend quality time, with each one of us.
- He is our *Dad*.
- He is powerful, and distinguished.
- He can be demanding, and entertaining.
- He is both far away, and very close.
- He is essential, and everlasting.
- He is genuine, and extremely brilliant.
- He is our Deliverer, and we praise his holy name.

- He is omnipotent, he is everywhere at once.
- He is; highly determined.
- He is; simple and complex.
- He is; rejuvenating and profound.
- He is; skilled and the greatest artist, who ever lived.
- He is very precise, he looks like a perfectionist.
- He is radiant, and very talented.
- He is polished.
- He drives you, in order to save you.
- He is shocking, and supernatural.
- He is a motivator.
- He is calm and joyful.
- He is love.
- He is very fast, and bright.
- He is altogether lovely.
- He is stern, for our safety.
- He is giving, and tenderly forgiving.
- He is funny.
- He is "The Genius."
- He is amazing.
- He is our "Trainer and Baptizer."

- He is smart.
- He is the "Redeemer and the Captain," of the team.
- He is the Fountain of Life.
- He is our healer, and joy giver.
- He gives purpose and meaning to life; because of truth.
- He is radical, and contagiously enthusiastic.
- He takes you; through the mountains.
- He sees you; over the hills.
- He refines you; in the fire.
- He holds you; with his grace.
- He keeps you; with his love.
- He is peace, and joy.
- He owns everything. "*Everything under Heaven belongs To God.*" (JOB 41:11)
- He is the way through, the road called life.
- He is the truth; we have always needed, and wanted to know.
- He is the life, we have always dreamed of.
- He is the door, Heaven will open.
- He is intense and awesome, completely full of all power; to help you.
- He is the Stairway into Heaven; *Jesus, The Christ*.
- He is the sign giver, the incredible miracle worker.

- He is the "Eye Doctor" letting us see him, and into the unseen realm.
- He is "The Designer, The Planner, The Architect and The Revealer."
- He is "El-Shaddai, Adonai and Yahweh."
- He is "The Great I Am."
- He is "The Alpha; The Beginning."
- He is "The Omega; The End."
- He is "The Bright & Morning Star."
- He is "Jehovah."
- He is the boss.
- He is protective.
- He is strong.
- He is a disciplinarian.
- He is Lord.
- He is spiritual.
- He is a Spirit.
- He is able to do everything, and anything.
- He cannot; fail.
- He is supreme, and stupendous.
- He is tenacious, and alluring.
- He is eternal.
- He is our teacher.

- He is sweet and kind.
- He is encouraging, and stands alongside of us.
- He is pure, and peaceful.
- He is our stabilizer.
- He is extravagant, and sincere.
- He is the commander in chief.
- He is the leader.
- He is the shame taker.
- He is our "High Priest," and intercessor.
- He prays; for us.
- He is *everything*.
- He is the highlight, of our life.
- He is capable, bold and wise.
- He is the same yesterday, today, and forever.
- He is *"The Father of Lights."*
- He never; changes.
- He is generous.
- He is "The King of Heaven."
- He is "The Sovereign Ruler, of The Universe."
- He is Hell's; worst nightmare.
- *It is He; who turns our hearts, toward Heaven.*

FOURTY ONE

IMPORTANT SCRIPTURES

The Bible is very clear on the fact, that without our obedience to Jesus Christ, we will perish. This was the major, missing piece of truth in my life. Please take the time to read over these scriptures, and obey the Lord. This will save your soul, for all eternity. Please remember that God loves you, and desires to keep you, absolutely – *forever*.

HEBREWS 5:8-9
"Though he were a Son, yet learned he obedience by the things which he suffered. 9And being made perfect, he became the author of eternal salvation unto all them that obey Him."

2 THESSALONIANS 1:7-9
"And to you who are troubled rest with us, when the Lord Jesus shall be revealed from Heaven with his mighty angels, 8 In flaming fire taking vengeance on them that Know not God, and that Obey not the Gospel of our Lord Jesus Christ: 9 Who shall be punished with everlasting

destruction from the presence of the Lord, and from the glory of his power."

HEBREWS 10:26-29

"For if we sin willfully after that we have received the knowledge of the truth, there remaineth no more sacrifice for sins, 27 But a certain fearful looking for of Judgment and Fiery Indignation, which shall devour the adversaries. 28 He that despised Moses' law died without mercy under two or three witnesses: 29 Of how much sorer punishment, suppose ye, shall he be thought worthy, who hath trodden underfoot the Son of God, and hath counted the blood of the covenant, wherewith he was sanctified, an unholy thing, and hath done despite unto the Spirit of Grace?"

JUDE 1:5

"I will therefore put you in remembrance, though ye once knew this, how that the Lord, having saved the people out of the land of Egypt, afterward destroyed them that believed not."

HEBREWS 3:5-6

"And Moses verily was faithful in all his house, as a servant, for a testimony of those things which were to be spoken after; 6 But Christ as a son over his own house; whose house are we, if we hold fast the confidence and the rejoicing of the hope firm unto the end."

MATTHEW 24:13

"But he that shall endure unto the end, the same shall be saved."

REVELATION 2:11

"He that hath an ear, let him hear what the Spirit saith unto the churches; He that Overcometh shall not be hurt of the second death."

REVELATION 18:1-4

"And after these things I saw another angel come down from Heaven, having great power; and the earth was lightened with his glory. 2 And he cried mightily with a strong voice, saying, Babylon the great is fallen, is fallen, and is become the habitation of devils, and the hold of every foul spirit, and a cage of every unclean and hateful bird. 3 For all nations have drunk of the wine of the wrath of her fornication, and the kings of the earth have committed fornication with her, and the merchants of the earth are waxed rich through the abundance of her delicacies. 4 And I heard another voice from Heaven, saying, Come out of her, My people, that ye be not partakers of her sins, and that ye receive not of her plagues."

EZEKIEL 18:4

"Behold, all souls are mine; as the soul of the father, so also the soul of the son is mine: the soul that sinneth, It shall die."

AMOS 9:10

"All the sinners of My people shall die by the sword, which say, The evil shall not overtake nor prevent us."

1 TIMOTHY 4:16

"Take heed unto thyself, and unto the doctrine; Continue in them: for in doing this thou shalt both save thyself, and them that hear thee."

JOHN 13:8

"Jesus answered him, If I wash thee not, thou hast no part with me."

1 CORINTHIANS 3:16-17

"Know ye not that ye are the temple of God, and that the Spirit of God dwelleth in you? 17 If any man defile the temple of God, him shall God destroy; for the temple of God is holy, which temple ye are."

MATHEW 13:41-42

"The Son of Man shall send forth his angels, and they shall gather out of His Kingdom all things that offend, and them which do iniquity; 42And shall cast them into a furnace of fire: there shall be wailing and gnashing of teeth."

1 CORINTHIANS 6:9-10

"Know ye not that the unrighteous shall not inherit the Kingdom of God? Be not deceived: neither fornicators, nor idolaters, nor adulterers, nor effeminate, nor abusers of themselves with mankind, 10 Nor thieves, nor covetous, nor drunkards, nor revilers, nor extortioners, shall inherit the Kingdom of God."

Wishing You A Beautiful Journey, With Jesus.

boots and lipstick

Enjoy Ann's sequel to "Real God."
Ann relays her divorce, deliverance and come back.
With God; you will rise.

the road up

Enjoy this sequel to "Real God" and "Boots & Lipstick."
This is a story of God's ability to bring victory; from tragedy.
With God; you will succeed.

WWW.REALORON.ORG